D1246452

A TAPESTRY OF
DAILY PRAYER

ABOUT THE COMPILER Patricia Newland obtained an Arts degree and a post-graduate diploma in Social Studies from Edinburgh University in the 1950s. She was licensed as a Reader in the Church of England in the Ely Diocese in 1980. Since that time she has been involved with the communication of the Christian Gospel through pastoral care, leading worship and through teaching. A Tapestry of Daily Prayer has been written for all those who wish help and guidance in their personal daily prayers.

ABOUT THE ILLUSTRATOR Joanna Queen obtained a Higher National Diploma in Illustration from the Cambridge College of Arts and Technology in 1987. Since then she has been doing freelance illustration with a particular emphasis on Christian communication.

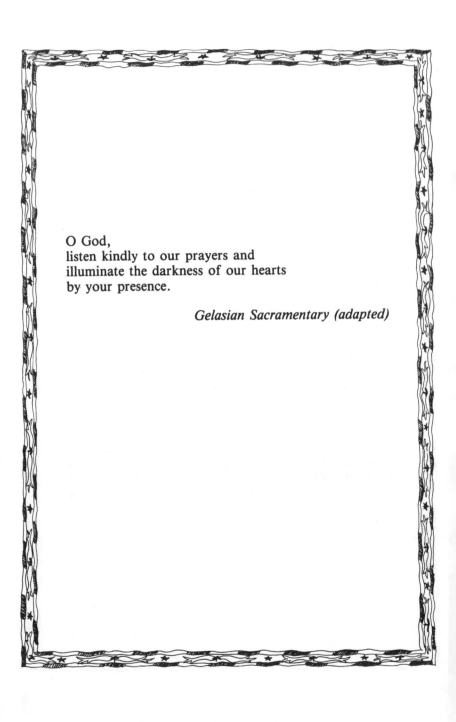

O God,
listen kindly to our prayers and
illuminate the darkness of our hearts
by your presence.

Gelasian Sacramentary (adapted)

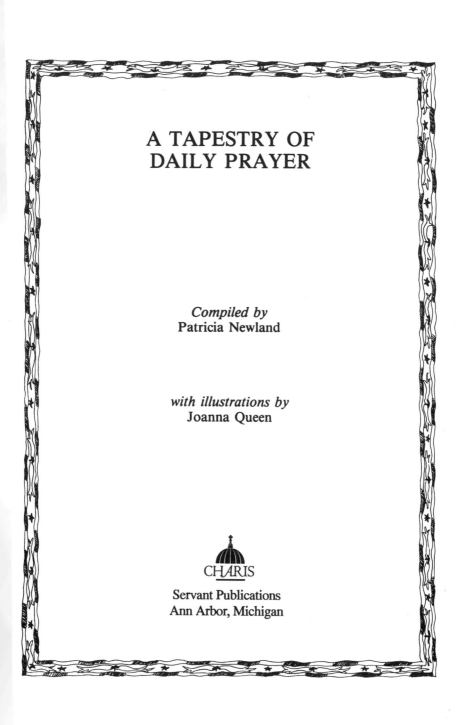

A TAPESTRY OF
DAILY PRAYER

Compiled by
Patricia Newland

with illustrations by
Joanna Queen

CHARIS

Servant Publications
Ann Arbor, Michigan

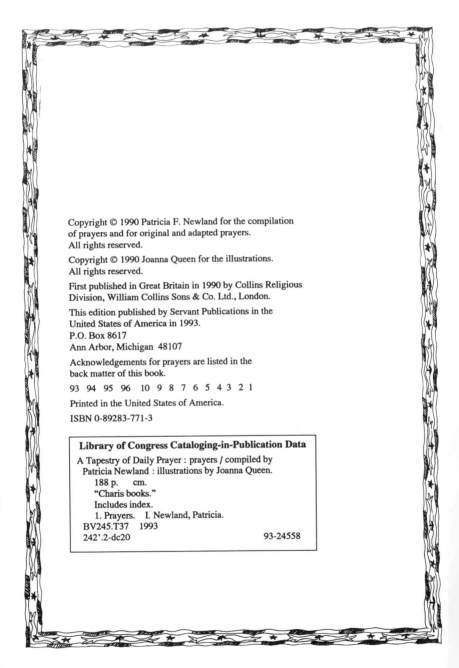

First published in Great Britain in 1990 by Collins Religious
Division, William Collins Sons & Co. Ltd., London.

This edition published by Servant Publications in the
United States of America in 1993.
P.O. Box 8617
Ann Arbor, Michigan 48107

Acknowledgements for prayers are listed in the
back matter of this book.

93 94 95 96   10 9 8 7 6 5 4 3 2 1

Printed in the United States of America.

ISBN 0-89283-771-3

Library of Congress Cataloging-in-Publication Data

A Tapestry of Daily Prayer : prayers / compiled by
  Patricia Newland : illustrations by Joanna Queen.
      188 p.   cm.
      "Charis books."
      Includes index.
      1. Prayers.   I. Newland, Patricia.
BV245.T37   1993
242'.2-dc20   93-24558

CONTENTS

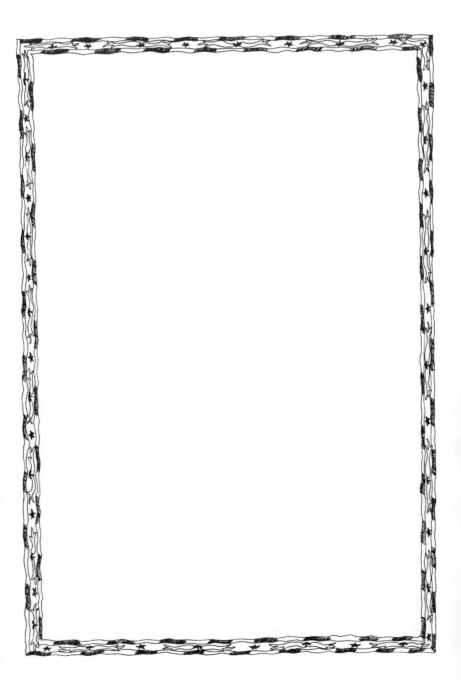

JANUARY

We saw his star, and we have come to worship him (Matthew 2 : 2)

1st   **Entrusting myself to God**

O eternal God,
Help me to trust my past to your
mercy, my future to your providence
and my present to your love, Amen.

After St. Augustine

January

2nd   **For help in prayer**

O God Supreme!
most secret and most present, most
beautiful and strong!
What shall I say, my God, my Life, my
Holy Joy?
What can I say when I speak of you?

St. Augustine

3rd   **Let nothing dismay me**

God made me.
God loves me and keeps me,
gives comfort and grace
for every need, at every moment,
in and around me, within me.
Thanks be to God.

Bishop George Appleton

4th   **For God's wisdom**

O God,
grant me serenity to accept the
things I cannot change,
courage to change the things I can,
and wisdom to know the difference.

Reinhold Niebuhr

5th   **For sharing God's love**

Dear Lord,
help me to spread thy fragrance
everywhere I go. Flood my soul with
thy spirit and life. Penetrate and
possess my whole being so utterly
that all my life may only be a
radiance of thine. Shine through me,
and be so in me that every soul I
come in contact with may feel thy
presence in my soul.

*Adapted by Mother Teresa from
a prayer by Cardinal Newman*

6th   **At Epiphany**

Almighty and everlasting God,
the brightness of all who believe,
who made known your only Son, our
Lord Jesus Christ, as the true light
of the world, fill the world with
your glory and show yourself by the
radiance of your light to all
peoples of the world, for the sake
of your Son, our Lord Jesus Christ,
Amen.

Gregorian Sacramentary (adapted)

7th   **For God's grace**

O God, the giver of all good things,
give me grace that I may work your
will, speak your words and walk in
your way, profound and calm like
waters deep and still.

Christina Rossetti (adapted)

8th   **For daily protection**

Defend me, O God, with your heavenly
grace, that I may continue yours for
ever and daily increase in your Holy
Spirit more and more, until I come to
your eternal kingdom, through
Jesus Christ our Lord, Amen.

Book of Common Prayer (adapted)

9th   **For God's guidance**

O God,
have mercy upon me.
You know my needs; teach me how to
feel them.
You know my ignorance; teach me how
to pray.
You know my weaknesses; teach me how
to look to you for strength.

Bishop Westcott (adapted)

10th **For God's love**

O God,
grant that I may not, for one moment,
admit willingly into my soul any
thought contrary to your love, for
Christ's sake, Amen.

E. B. Pusey

11th **Morning Commendation**

O God,
who has brought me from the rest of
last night into the joyous light of
this day,
bring me from the new light of this
day into the guiding light of
eternity.
Oh! from the new light of this day
into the guiding light of eternity.

Gaelic (adapted)

12th **For personal help**

I am silent, Lord, in my affliction.
I am silent. In the stillness of a
contrite and humble heart, I listen
to you.

I am silent. I suffer. I worship
silently. Yet you hear my sighs, and
the pain of my heart is not hidden
from you. Let me not listen to
myself. I long to hear your voice.

François Fénelon (adapted)

13th   **For complete trust in God**

O my God,
give me such confidence, such
peace, such happiness in you,
that your will may always be
dearer to me than my own will,
and your pleasure than my own
pleasure.

All that you give is your free
gift to me. All that you take
away is your grace to me. Let
me thank you for all, praise you
for all and love you for all,
through Jesus Christ our Lord,
Amen.

Christina Rossetti (adapted)

14th   **Commendation at night**

O merciful God,
be present and protect us through the
silent hours of this night, so that
we who are wearied by the changes and
chances of this life on earth may
rest upon your eternal
changelessness.

Leonine Sacramentary (adapted)

15th   Commendation

We commend to you, Lord,
our souls and our bodies,
our minds and our thoughts,
our prayers and our hopes,
our health and our work,
our life and our death;
our partner in life,
our parents, brothers, sisters,
children, friends,
and all in need,
this day and always, Amen.

Lancelot Andrewes (adapted)

16th   For God's help in pain

The worst of pain, O Lord, is that it
makes it difficult to pray.
Yet, O Lord, I desire to pray, to
have communion with you, to draw
strength and healing from you, to
link to you those whom I love and
those who need your love,
to thank you for those who look after
me and those who wish me well.
O Lord, let me always remember that
to talk to you is prayer.

Bishop George Appleton

17th   The Jesus Prayer

Lord Jesus Christ,
Son of the living God,
have mercy on me, a sinner.

An anonymous prayer from Russia

January

18th   **For God's daily grace**

Lord Jesus,
give me daily grace for my daily need;
daily patience for my daily cross;
daily, hourly, incessant love for you,
so that I may take up your cross
daily and carry it for you.

Christina Rossetti (adapted)

19th   **The Lord's Prayer**

O God, my loving father,
may I love you and honour you.

Fill me with the joy and peace of
knowing that you love me, so that
I may be in heaven here on earth.

Give me the food that I need for today.

Forgive me my selfishness and help me
to forgive those who have hurt me.

Strengthen me in testing times and
keep me out of harm's way.

For you, O God, are the giver of all
love and life, now and for ever,
Amen.

P. N.

20th   **For the good use of my life**
O God,
make me remember that every day is
your gift and ought to be used
according to your command, through
Jesus Christ our Lord, Amen.

Samuel Johnson

21st   **For laughter**
O God, my Friend,
help me to laugh at myself,
to laugh with others and
to have your joy in my heart, Amen.

P. N.

22nd   **For inner peace**
Lord Jesus, Prince of Peace,
teach me to see my daily life in the
context of my eternal life.
Lighten my daily load.
Reconcile me to your will and give me
that peace that the world cannot take
away, Amen.

Dr Chalmers (adapted)

23rd   **Personal prayer**
O loving and eternal God,
who longs to be the heart of my
heart, the strength of my strength
and the love of my life, help me to
receive you joyfully into my life and
come to know you better every day,
Amen.

P. N.

24th   **Commendation**

O God, loving friend and helper,
use the loose ends of my life in your
plan of salvation.
Take my failures, my pains and my
fears, and transform them for use in
your kingdom, for Jesus Christ's
sake, Amen.

P. N.

25th   **Celebrating St Paul's conversion**

Lord Christ,
who met your apostle Paul on the road
to Damascus and brought him from
darkness to light and from hate to
love, help me to a life of light and
love, that I may live always for your
sake, Amen.

P. N.

26th   **For our friends**

O God, Fountain of Love,
love our friends and teach them to
love you with all their hearts, that
they may think and speak and do only
those things that please you, for
Jesus Christ's sake, Amen.

St. Anselm (adapted)

27th **For personal help**

O God,
help of the helpless,
cure my infirmities,
forgive my offences,
lighten my burdens,
enrich my poverty,
through Jesus Christ our Lord, Amen.

Dr Sutton

28th **For Christ's companionship**

O Christ, my only Saviour,
so dwell within me that I may go
forward with the light of hope in my
eyes, the fire of inspiration on my
lips, your word on my tongue and your
love in my heart, Amen.

Unknown

29th **Confession**

O merciful God,
I admit to you my numerous
shortcomings. Forgive me, for the
love of Christ.
O God our Father,
never let me be without the
indwelling of your Holy Spirit.
Let my life be every day less
conscious of myself and more
conscious of you, Amen.

Dr Norman Macleod (adapted)

30th   **For commitment to God's service**

Here I am, Lord, –
body, heart and soul.
Grant that with your love, I may be
big enough to reach the world and
small enough to be at one with you.

Co-workers of Mother Teresa

31st   **For God's blessing**

All loving God,
bless all who worship you.
Of your goodness, give us.
With your love inspire us.
By your Spirit guide us.
By your power protect us.
In your mercy receive us now and
always, Amen.

An ancient collect

*You can be sure that whoever gives even
a drink of cold water to one of the least of
these my followers because he is my
follower, will certainly receive a reward.*
(Matthew 10 : 42)

1st   **For compassion**

Lord,
shake away my indifference and
insensitivity to the plight of the poor.
When I meet you hungry, thirsty, or
as a stranger, show me how I can give
you food or quench your thirst or
receive you in my home – and in my
heart. Show me how I can serve you
in the least of your brothers or
sisters, Amen.

Co-workers of Mother Teresa

2nd   **At Candlemas**

O God,
we thank you that your Son, our Lord
Jesus Christ, was presented in the
Temple. We thank you that Simeon and
Anna saw him as the light of our
salvation, a sign of hope and peace.

Give to us a sure and perfect faith
in him, that we may live our lives to
your glory, for your love's sake,
Amen.

P. N.

February

3rd   **Who are the poor?**

The poor are the materially and
spiritually destitute.
The poor are the hungry and the
thirsty.
The poor are those who need clothing.
The poor are the homeless and the
harbourless.
The poor are the sick.
The poor are the physically and
mentally handicapped.
The poor are the aged.
The poor are those imprisoned.
The poor are the lonely.
The poor are the ignorant and the
doubtful.
The poor are the sorrowful.
The poor are the comfortless.
The poor are the helpless.
The poor are the persecuted.
The poor are those who suffer
injustice.
The poor are the ill-mannered.
The poor are the bad-tempered.
The poor are the sinners and
scoffers.
The poor are those who do us wrong.
The poor are the unwanted, the
outcasts of society.
The poor are somehow or other —
we ourselves.

Co-workers of Mother Teresa

4th   **For the destitute**

O God of Love,
who sees all the suffering, injustice
and misery in the world, have pity on
all in need. Fill our hearts with
deep compassion for those who suffer,
for the sake of Jesus Christ our
Lord, Amen.

Eugène Bersier (adapted)

5th   **For the hungry and thirsty**

Almighty and everlasting God,
the comfort of the sad and the
strength of sufferers, hear the
prayers of those who cry out to you
for material and spiritual help.
Let them rejoice to find your love
and mercy present in their suffering,
through Jesus Christ our Lord, Amen.

Gelasian Sacramentary (adapted)

6th   **For those who need clothing**

O God, our merciful Father,
pity those who are in need of
clothing for their bodies. Give them
clothes to wear and clothe them also
in your Holy Spirit,
for your love's sake, Amen.

P. N.

February

7th   **For the homeless and the harbourless**

Lord Jesus,
we pray for the homeless and
the starving,
for the sick and the wounded,
for the dying and those without hope.

Save and comfort all who suffer and
be closest of all to those who need
you most, Amen.

P. N.

8th   **For the sick**

O our Master, Jesus Christ,
visit the sick of your people and
heal them, Amen.

Abyssinian Jacobite Liturgy

9th **For the handicapped**

Lord Jesus,
We bring to you for help those who
are handicapped in body or mind.
Relieve their distress.
Give them faith in your love.
Give them hope as they learn to live
with their disabilities, and give
them the joy and support of love and
friendship, now and always, Amen.

P. N.

10th **For the aged**

God of Love,
whose compassion never fails,
we bring to you the needs of all who
are elderly:
the pains of those who are sick or
infirm; the sorrows and loneliness
of the bereaved; the deprivations of
the neglected; the worries of the
anxious; the helplessness of the
weak.
Strengthen and relieve them, Father,
according to their various needs and
your great mercy, for the sake of
your Son our Saviour Jesus Christ,
Amen.

St. Anselm (adapted)

11th   **For those imprisoned**

O God,
who alone has the power to set us
free, we pray for those in prison:
Sustain in hope and courage those who
are imprisoned on account of their faith
or for crimes that they did not commit;
Help those who have deserved their
imprisonment to prepare for a new life
in the ways of justice and love;
for Jesus Christ's sake, Amen.

P. N.

12th   **For the lonely**

Loving God,
pour the balm of your comfort on
those who are lonely. Have pity on
those who are bereft of human love
and on those to whom it has never
come. Be to them a strong
consolation and give them fullness of
joy, for the sake of Jesus Christ,
your Son, our Lord, Amen.

Anonymous

13th   **For the doubtful**

Know you for your comfort that the
world is God's and without him is
nothing that is made.
Know you when you weep for the world
that God knows its every sorrow, its
every need, its every frailty.
Know you when you tremble for the
world that God is the Mighty One,
with power and compassion beyond our
dreams.
Know you when you labour for the
world that God is with you always,
even unto the end.
Take great comfort, God is not gone
away. Yet hasten, God waits upon
you.

Alan Paton

14th   **For those who mourn**

Loving and tender Father,
comfort those who mourn.
Console them in their grief.
Strengthen them in their sorrow.
Help them to express their love for
those who have died by their
friendship and service to others.

P. N.

February

15th   **For the comfortless**

O merciful God,
comfort in their tribulation those
who lack comfort.
Help them when the world seems empty
of your presence and no word comes
to reassure their hearts.
Reassure them in the darkness, that
they may wait patiently for the
light, and in the silence listen for
your voice, and in all things trust
your promises in Jesus Christ our
Lord.

New Every Morning (adapted)

16th   **For the helpless**

O God,
the refuge of the poor, the strength
of those who toil, and the comforter
of all who sorrow, we commend to your
mercy the unfortunate and needy in
whatever land they may be. You alone
know the number and extent of their
sufferings and trials.
Look down, Father of Mercies, at
those unhappy families suffering from
war and slaughter, from hunger and
disease, and other severe trials.
Spare them, O Lord, for it is truly a
time for mercy.

Peter Canisius

17th   **For the persecuted**

O God, our mighty Deliverer,
help and defend us.
Rescue the oppressed;
Pity the insignificant;
Raise the fallen;
Show yourself to the needy;
Heal the sick;
Bring back those of your people who
have gone astray;
Feed the hungry;
Lift up the weak and take off the
prisoners' chains.

May every nation come to know that
you alone are God and that all
mankind are your children.

St Clement of Rome (adapted)

18th   **For those who suffer injustice**

O God,
baptise our hearts into a sense of
the needs and conditions of all, so
we may fervently seek the common
good, for your love's sake, Amen.

George Fox (adapted)

19th **For the ill-mannered**

Most merciful Father,
have mercy on all who are ill-
mannered and who have brought trouble
and punishment on themselves.
Have mercy on those who have injured
others by their thoughtlessness.
Give them this day a sign of your
grace and an opportunity to change,
for your mercy's sake, Amen.

P. N.

20th **For the bad-tempered**

O God,
help me to pray for those with bad
tempers whom I find difficult to
love.

O God,
you return gladly and lovingly to
lift up the one who offends you and
I do not turn to raise up and honour
the one who angers me.

O God, help me.

St John of the Cross (adapted)

21st   **For sinners and scoffers**

Lord Jesus, who came to save sinners,
we pray for criminals who need
desperately to know your love.
We pray for all addicts and
frightened people.
We pray for all who scoff at
Christians.
We pray for all your unhappy people.

Help all in need to turn to you, so
that hate may become love, fear may
become trust and despair may become
hope and joy.

P. N.

22nd   **For those who do us wrong**

O Lord,
remember not only the men and women
of goodwill,
but also those of ill will.
But do not remember only the
suffering they have inflicted upon us,
remember the fruits we bought thanks
to this suffering,
our comradeship, our loyalty, our
humility,
the courage, the generosity, the
greatness of heart which has grown
out of all this.
And when they come to judgement, let
all the fruits that we have borne be
their forgiveness.
AMEN AMEN AMEN

(Written on a piece of wrapping paper
near the body of a dead child in
Ravensbrück where 92,000 women and
children died)

23rd   **For the outcasts of society**

O God, creator of all things,
who made us in your image, help those
who feel unwanted to find joy and
satisfaction in their daily lives.
Help them to come to know that they
are both needed and loved, through
Jesus Christ our Lord, Amen.

P. N.

24th   **For myself**

O God, who always loves me,
I give to you all that is hurtful in
my life.
I give you my pain.
I give you my rejections.
I give you my bitterness.
I give you my selfishness.
I give you my pride.
I give you my fears.
I give you my grief.
I give you my longings.
Help me to give all these,
together with my love, into your
safe-keeping, Amen.

P. N.

25th   **For those who minister**

Lord Jesus Christ,
who alone has power over life and
death, over health and sickness, give
power, wisdom and gentleness to all
your ministering servants.

May they always bear your presence
with them, that they may not only
heal but bless, and shine as lamps of
hope in the darkest hours of distress
and fear.

Lord, in your mercy, hear our prayer,
Amen.

*Society for the Propagation of
the Gospel (adapted)*

26th   **For the rich and influential**

O loving God,
we pray to you for all those to whom
you have given positions of influence
in the world. May they praise you
with their lives and honour you with
their wealth. May they by their
example induce others to seek for
that imperishable inheritance which
your beloved Son, our Lord Jesus,
will give to all who have followed
him in meekness, purity and faith,
through the same Jesus Christ our
Lord, Amen,

R. M. Benson

27th   **For help in the service of others**

O Divine master,
grant that I may seek not so much
to be consoled as to console,
not so much to be understood as to understand,
not so much to be loved as to love;
for it is in giving that we receive,
it is in pardoning that we are pardoned,
it is in dying that we awake to eternal life.

Attributed to St Francis of Assissi

28th   **For faith in the midst of suffering**

Lord,
I have found you in the terrible
magnitude of the suffering of others.
I have seen you in the sublime
acceptance and unaccountable joy of
those whose lives are racked with
pain. I have heard your voice in the
words of those whose personal agony
mysteriously increases their selfless
concern for other people.

But in my niggling aches and petty
sorrows I have failed to find you.
I have lost the drama of your great
redemptive passion in my own mundane
weariness. The joyful life of Easter
is submerged in the drabness of self-
preoccupation.

Lord,
hear my prayer and let my cry come
unto you.

Co-workers of Mother Teresa

29th   **General intercession**

Into your hands, O Lord our God,
we commend ourselves and all who need
your pity and protection.
Enlighten us with your heavenly grace
and never let us be separated from
you, O God in Trinity, O God Eternal.

St Edmund of Abingdon (adapted)

MARCH

God loved the world so much that he gave
his only Son, so that everyone who
believes in him may not die but have
eternal life.   (John 3 : 16)

1st　　**Saint David's day**

O God our Father,
we thank you for the inspired
leadership of David, Bishop of Wales.
Help us, like him, to be fervent
in prayer, to encourage others in
faith, and always to follow your way
of the Cross, for your love's sake, Amen.

P. N.

2nd　　**Christ's words in Gethsemane**

'Abba, Father, all things are
possible to you. Remove this cup
from me, yet not what I will, but
what you will.'

Mark 14 : 36

3rd　　**Christ's words at the nailing on the Cross**

'Father, forgive them, for they know
not what they do.'

Luke 23 : 34

4th　　**Christ's words, dying on the Cross**

'My God, my God, why have you
forsaken me?'

Mark 15 : 34

March

5th　　　**Christ's words, at the moment of death**

'Father,
into your hands I commit my spirit.'

Luke 23 : 46

6th　　　**Thanks to Christ**

Thanks be to you, my Lord Jesus
Christ, for all the benefits which
you have given me and for all the
pains and insults you have borne for
me.

St Richard of Chichester

7th　　　**On receiving Holy Communion**

Almighty Father,
whose dear Son, on the night before
he died, instituted the Sacrament of
his Body and Blood; help us to
receive these gifts of bread and wine
thankfully, in remembrance of him,
who in these holy mysteries gives us
a pledge of eternal life, your Son
our Saviour Jesus Christ, Amen.

American Prayer Book (adapted)

8th   **For grace**

O God,
give us grace, by constant obedience,
to offer up our wills and hearts to
you as an acceptable sacrifice,
through Jesus Christ our Lord, Amen.

Christina Rossetti (adapted)

9th   **For faithfulness**

O Lord our Saviour,
You have told us that you will
require much from those to whom much
is given.
Help your followers to unite together
in prayer and in service to others,
for the increase of your kingdom,
Amen.

P. N.

10th   **For our daily spiritual needs**

O Lord God Almighty,
in your great love to us, give us a
spirit of love to you and a
compassionate heart to all in need.
In every difficulty, be our guide.
In testing times, be our defence.
In weakness, be our strength and in
weariness be our rest, for your great
love's sake, Amen.

Manual of the Guild of St Barnabas
(adapted)

March

11th   **A memorial of Christ's Passion**

Lord Jesus,
who died on the Cross for our
salvation, enable us to deny
ourselves and to spend and be spent
in your service. Help us to take up
our Cross daily and give us grace to
glorify your name, Amen.

G. Calthrop (adapted)

12th   **For the inspiration of God's Holy
Spirit**

Almighty God,
unto whom all hearts are open, all
desires known and from whom no
secrets are hidden; cleanse the
thoughts of our hearts by the
inspiration of your Holy Spirit, that
we may perfectly love you and praise
your holy name, through Jesus Christ
our Lord, Amen.

Gregorian Sacramentary (adapted)

13th   **Memorial to Christ's Passion**

O Lord Jesus Christ,
who suffered death on the Cross for
us, forgive us all our sins, cleanse
us and make us pure.
O Lord Jesus Christ,
who died so that we might live, let
us not grieve you by our sins, but
soften our hard hearts and bend our
wills, that we may hear your voice
and live, Amen.

H. W. Turner (adapted)

14th   **For Christ's forgiveness**

O Lord Jesus Christ,
who for our sake bore bitter
suffering and does not send us more
than we are able to bear, give us
help and strength to bear patiently
all our troubles. Help us to learn
also to forgive, as we hope ourselves
to be forgiven, for your love's sake,
Amen.

H. W. Turner

15th   **For dependence on God**

O God, our Help and Strength,
grant that when we are tempted, we
may resist the devil;
that when we are worried, we may cast
all our care upon you;
that when we are weary, we may seek
your rest and that in all things we
may live this day to your glory,
Amen.

Source unknown

16th   **For those in temptation**

O God, most Holy Spirit,
give your strength to those who are
tried by any special temptation.
Help them to stand firm in your faith
and sustain them so that they may be
able to triumph over it.

The Narrow Way (adapted)

March

17th   **On St Patrick's Day**

Christ be with me,
Christ before me,
Christ behind me,
Christ within me,
Christ beneath me,
Christ above me,
Christ on my right,
Christ on my left,
Christ where I lie,
Christ where I sit,
Christ where I arise,
Christ in the heart of everyone who
thinks of me,
Christ in the mouth of everyone who
speaks of me,
Christ in every eye that sees me,
Christ in every ear that hears me.

Salvation is of the Lord,
Salvation is of the Lord,
Salvation is of the Christ,
May your salvation, O Lord, be ever
with us, Amen.

St Patrick

18th   For faith in suffering

O my Lord Jesus,
I believe, and by your grace will
ever believe and hold, and I know
that it is true, and will be true to
the end of the world, that nothing
great is done without suffering,
without humiliation, and that all
things are possible by means of it.
Help me to be patient when sorrow or
pain is prolonged, for the love of
you and of your Cross.

Cardinal Newman

19th   For knowing God's love

O Christ,
give us patience, faith and hope as
we kneel at the foot of your Cross
and hold fast to it. Teach us by
your Cross, that however badly things
seem to us, the Father so loves us
that he spared not you.

Charles Kingsley

20th   On St Cuthbert's Day

Almighty God,
who called your servant Cuthbert from
keeping sheep to follow your Son and
be a shepherd of your people,
mercifully grant that we, following
his example and caring for those who
are lost, may bring them home to your
fold, through Jesus Christ our Lord,
Amen.

Prayer used in Durham Cathedral

March

21st   **Thirsting for Christ**

O Blessed Jesus, our Lord and Master,
who was pleased to thirst for our
souls, help us not to be satisfied
with the pleasure of this life, but
always to thirst for the salvation of
the souls you died to save, and above
all to thirst for you, for your
love's sake, Amen.

Bishop Edward King

22nd   **For the love of Christ**

O Christ,
by the memory of your Cross's
hallowed and most bitter anguish,
make us reverence you and make us
love you, Amen.

St Bridget (adapted)

23rd   **Meditation on Christ's Cross**

O my sweet Saviour Christ,
who in your undeserved love towards
us was prepared to suffer the painful
death of the Cross, suffer me not to
be cold or lukewarm in my love
towards you.

St Thomas More

24th   **Learning from Christ's Cross**

O Christ, my Lord,
who for my sins did hang upon a tree,
grant that your grace in me, poor
wretch, may still ingrafted be.

Philip Howard (abridged)

25th   **On Lady Day**

O most loving Mary,
most glorious mother of faithfulness
and love, we give thanks that you
were able to nurture and raise our
Lord Jesus and stay with him
to the end.
Help us also to be humble, loving and
faithful in our response to God, that
our Lord Jesus Christ may live and
grow in our hearts now and in
eternity, Amen.

P. N.

March

26th   **Adoration of Christ**

O Christ,
I kiss the wounds in your sacred
head, with sorrow deep and true,
may every thought of mine this day
be an act of love for you.

I kiss the wounds in your sacred
hands, with sorrow deep and true,
may every touch of my hands this day
be an act of love for you.

I kiss the wounds in your sacred
feet, with sorrow deep and true,
may every step I take this day
be an act of love for you.

I kiss the wounds in your sacred
side, with sorrow deep and true,
may every beat of my heart this day
be an act of love for you.

George Spencer

27th   **In the testing of faith**

O Lord Jesus Christ,
look upon us with those eyes of
yours, the eyes with which you looked
upon Peter in the hall of judgement,
so that with Peter we may repent and
by your great love be forgiven and
restored, for your mercy's sake,
Amen.

Lancelot Andrewes

28th   **Meditation on the Cross**

Lord Jesus,
who stretched out your arms of love
on the hard wood of the Cross, that
all might come within the reach of
your saving embrace, clothe us in
your spirit, that we, stretching out
our hands in loving labour for others,
may bring those who know you not,
to knowledge and love of you,
who with the Father and the Holy
Spirit lives and reigns one God,
Amen.

Charles H. Brent

29th   **Meditation on the Cross**

Lord Jesus, our Saviour,
let us now come to you.

Our hearts are cold; Lord, warm them
with your selfless love.
Our hearts are sinful; Lord, cleanse
them with your precious blood.
Our hearts are weak; Lord, strengthen
them with your joyous spirit.
Our hearts are empty; Lord, fill
them with your divine presence.
Lord Jesus, our hearts are yours;
possess them always and only for
yourself, Amen.

St Augustine

March

30th   **Prayer to Christ**

O Lord,
remember me, now you are in your
kingdom, for your great love's sake,
Amen.

Luke 23:42 (adapted)

31st   **Adoration of Christ**

We adore you, O Christ, and we bless
you, because by your Cross you have
redeemed the world.

O Saviour of the world, who by your
Cross and precious Blood has
redeemed us, save us and help us, we
humbly beseech you, O our God.

Antiphons on Good Friday,
Western Rite

APRIL

He is not here; he has been raised.
(Luke 24 : 6)

1st   **For the blessing of faith**

Lord Jesus,
make your home in our hearts
through faith and help us to
understand how broad and long,
how high and deep, is your love
for each one of us, Amen.

Ephesians 3 : 17 - 18 (adapted)

2nd   **Thanksgiving for Christ's
Resurrection**

Blessed be the God and Father of our
Lord Jesus Christ! By his great
mercy, we have been born anew to a
living hope through the resurrection
of Jesus Christ from the dead. We
have an inheritance which is
imperishable, undefiled, unfading and
kept in heaven for us.

1 Peter 1 : 3 - 5 (adapted)

3rd   **For following Christ's Way**

O our Saviour,
You, who have loved us,
make us love you.
You who have sought us,
make us seek you.
Be to us the way, that we may find
you and be found in you, our only
hope and everlasting joy.

E. B. Pusey (abridged)

April

4th   **For being with God**

O my God,
shall I one day see you?
What sight can compare to that
great sight?
Shall I see the source of that grace
which enlightens me, strengthens me
and consoles me?
As I come from you, as I am made
through you, so O my God, may I at
last return to you and be with you
for ever and ever, Amen.

Cardinal Newman

5th   **For eternal life**

Eternal Light shine into our hearts.
Eternal Goodness deliver us from evil.
Eternal Power be our support.
Eternal Wisdom scatter the darkness
of our ignorance.
Eternal Pity have mercy on us, that
with all our heart and mind and
strength and soul we may seek your
face and be brought by your infinite
mercy to your holy presence, through
Jesus Christ our Lord, Amen.

Alcuin

6th   **For wisdom**

O gracious and holy Father,
give us wisdom to perceive you,
diligence to seek you,
patience to wait for you,
eyes to see you,
a heart to meditate on you
and a life to proclaim you,
through the power of the Spirit of
Jesus Christ our Lord, Amen.

St Benedict of Nursia

7th   **For faith in God**

O God, our most mighty Protector,
safe in your tender care, let us hope.
Let us believe in your support, both
when we are little and when we are old.
Let us understand that when our
strength is from you, it is real
strength, but when it springs from
our own efforts, it is weakness.

St. Augustine

8th   **For awareness of God**

O God,
give me a pure heart that I may
see you,
a humble heart that I may hear you,
a heart of love that I may serve you,
and a heart of faith that I may stay
with you.

Author unknown

April

9th   **For receiving God**

O God,
give us eyes to see you,
ears to hear you,
a will to look for you, and a
trusting heart to believe in you,
today and every day,
for Jesus Christ's sake, Amen.

P. N.

10th   **For joy in God**

O God,
who is the sun of righteousness and
light eternal, giving gladness to all
things, shine upon us now and ever,
that we may be glad and cheerful in
you, for Jesus Christ's sake, Amen.

Ancient Collect

11th   **For joy out of sorrow**

Most merciful God, helper of all, so
strengthen us by your power, that our
sorrows may be turned to joy, and we
may continually glorify your holy
name, through Jesus Christ
our Lord, Amen.

Sarum Breviary

12th   **For receiving God's Spirit**

O God, you are Spirit and Truth,
help us to worship you in spirit
and truth.
O God, you are Rest and Peace, help
us to be at rest and peace.
O God, you are Love and Humility,
help us to receive your love humbly
and share it with our neighbour.

P. N.

13th   **For walking in God's Spirit**

O heavenly Father, in whom we live
and move and have our being, so guide
and govern us by your Holy Spirit
that in all the cares and occupations
of our daily life we may never forget
you, but remember that we are always
walking in your sight.

Ancient collect (adapted)

April

14th   **For God's peace**

O God,
give peace between us and peace in
our hearts. May our voices proclaim
your truth and may your Cross be the
guardian of our souls, for your
love's sake, Amen.

Nestorian Liturgy (adapted)

15th   **For God's light**

O God,
listen kindly to our prayers and
illuminate the darkness of our hearts
by your presence, through Jesus
Christ our Lord, Amen.

Gelasian Sacramentary (adapted)

16th   **For God's guidance**

O God,
for as much as without you, we are
not able to please you, mercifully
grant that your Holy Spirit may in
all things direct and rule our
hearts, through Jesus Christ our
Lord, Amen.

Gelasian Sacramentary

17th   **For God's presence**

O God,
hear our prayers and give to us your
tender love, that we who are weighed
down by our personal cares may be
refreshed by the coming of our
Saviour, through the same Jesus
Christ, Amen.

Gelasian Sacramentary (adapted)

18th   **For knowledge of God's will**

God almighty, eternal, just and
merciful,
help us poor sinners to work in your
name and for your sake. Purify and
enlighten us with your Holy Spirit,
so that we may follow in the
footsteps of your Son, our Lord Jesus
Christ, Amen.

St. Francis of Assisi (adapted)

19th   **For unity and comfort**

O God of Peace,
unite our hearts by your bond of
peace, that we may be gentle with one
another and live in peace and unity.
O God of Patience,
give us patience in times of trial
and steadfastness to endure to the
end.

Bernhard Albrecht
(abridged and adapted)

April

20th   **For trust in the living God**

O God, whose way is perfect,
help us always to trust in your
goodness; that walking with you, we
may be contented and peaceful as we
cast every care upon you, knowing
that you care for us. Amen.

Christina Rossetti (adapted)

21st   **On St Anselm's Day**

O Lord my God,
teach my heart this day where and how
to see you, where and how to find
you. You have made me and re-made me
and you have given me all the good
things I possess and still I do not
know you.
I have not yet done that for which I
was made. Teach me to seek you, for
I cannot seek you unless you teach me.
Let me find you by loving you. Let
me love you when I find you.

St Anselm (abridged and adapted)

22nd   **For seeing God's glory**

O God,
we seek your face.
Turn to us and show us your glory,
then our longing shall be satisfied
and our peace shall be perfect,
through Jesus Christ our Lord, Amen.

St Augustine (abridged and adapted)

23rd   **For knowledge of Christ**

O Lord Jesus Christ, friend and
brother,
may I know you more clearly, love you
more dearly and follow you more
nearly.

St Richard of Chichester

24th   **For life with God**

O God, Holy Spirit,
give us for our blessing, thoughts
which pass into prayer, prayers which
pass into love, and love which passes
into life with you for ever, Amen.

New Every Morning (adapted)

April

25th   On St Mark's Day

O Lord and Master, Jesus Christ,
Word of the everlasting Father,
you have borne our griefs and carried
the burden of our weaknesses;
renew by your Spirit the gifts of
healing in your Church, and send out
your disciples again to proclaim the
good news of your kingdom, and to
cure the sick and relieve your
suffering children, to the praise and
glory of your holy name, Amen.

Liturgy of St Mark

26th   For Christ's presence

O God,
help us to feel your presence as
we pray.
Help us to trust that as Jesus
Christ, our Saviour, is raised with
you in glory, so too he is ever
present with us until the end of
time.

Leonine Sacramentary

27th   For protection from evil

Almighty God,
may we seek your protection from evil
and serve you in peace and quietness
of spirit, through Jesus Christ our
Lord, Amen.

Roman Breviary (adapted)

28th   **For union with God**

O God, Holy Spirit ever with us,
keep us close to you.
Let nothing separate us from you.
Let nothing keep us back from you,
If we fall, bring us back quickly
to you.
Make us hope in you, trust in you and
love you always, through Jesus Christ
our Lord, Amen.

E. B. Pusey (adapted)

29th   **For Christ to draw us to him**

O blessed Saviour,
Draw us by the cords of your love.
Draw us by the sense of your
goodness.
Draw us by yourself.
Draw us by the purity and beauty of
your example.
Draw us by the merit of your precious
death and by the power of your
Holy Spirit.
Draw us to you, good Lord, and we
shall run after you, Amen.

Isaac Barrow (adapted)

30th   **To give honour to God**

To you, O God, King eternal,
immortal, invisible, the only wise
God, be honour and glory for ever and
ever, Amen.

1 Timothy 1 : 17
(adapted)

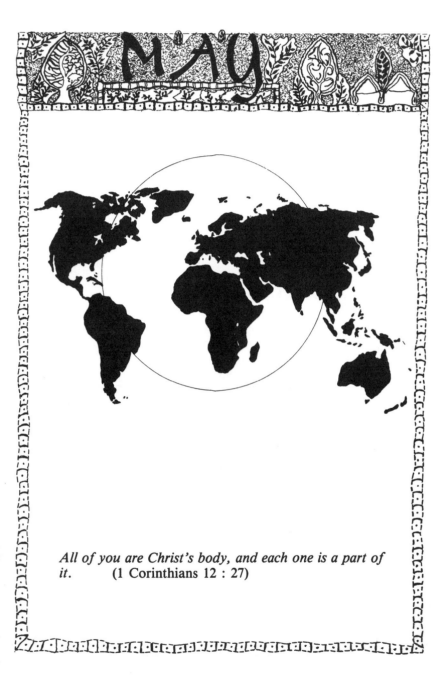

All of you are Christ's body, and each one is a part of it.   (1 Corinthians 12 : 27)

1st   **On St Philip's Day**

Lord Jesus Christ,
the Way, the Truth, and the Life;
let us not stray from you, the Way,
nor distrust you, the Truth, nor rest
in any other but you, the Life.
Teach us by your Holy Spirit what to
believe, what to do, and in what to
take our rest, for your love's sake,
Amen.

Erasmus

2nd   **For the imitation of Christ**

O God, who has given us your Son to
be an example and a help to our
weakness in following the path that
leads to life, help us to be his
disciples and tread in his footsteps,
Amen.

Roman Breviary

3rd   **For God's help in worship**

Almighty God,
whom the eye cannot see, whom the ear
cannot hear, let us this day feel
your presence and know your love.
Help us to worship you in spirit and
in truth, and may this spiritual
worship keep clear within us a
knowledge of your way, through Jesus
Christ our Lord, Amen.

George Dawson (adapted)

May

4th　　　　　**For the guidance of the Church**

We pray you, Lord, to direct and
guide your Church with your unfailing
care, that it may be vigilant in time
of quiet and daring in time of
trouble, Amen.

Franciscan Breviary

5th　　　　　**For Christ's presence with us**

Loving Lord Jesus,
As you accompanied those two
disciples on the road to Emmaus, be
also with us on our journey of life.
Guide us, strengthen us and make our
hearts to burn with love for you.
Make us always aware of the power of
your presence within us, for your
love's sake, Amen.

Archdeacon of Raphoe

6th   **For receiving God's Holy Spirit**

O Holy Spirit of God,
who on the day of Pentecost came to
the believers in wind and fire,
come to us today.

O Holy Spirit of God,
who on the day of Pentecost filled
the believers with new courage and
faith as followers of Christ,
come to us today.

O Holy Spirit of God,
our guide, comforter and friend,
come to us today.

P. N.

7th   **For the Church**

Most gracious Father,
we pray for your Church.
Fill it with all truth.
Where it is corrupt, purge it.
Where it is in error, direct it.
Where anything is amiss, reform it.
Where it is right,
strengthen and confirm it.
Where it is in want, furnish it.
Where it is divided, heal it and
unite it in your love,
through Jesus Christ our Lord, Amen.

Archbishop Laud (adapted)

May

8th   **For receiving God**

O God,
of your goodness, give me yourself;
for you are sufficient for me.
I cannot properly ask anything less,
to be worthy of you. If I were to
ask less, I should always be in want.
In you alone do I have all.

Julian of Norwich

9th   **For increase in faith and trust**

Lord Jesus,
I am weak in faith; strengthen me.
I am cold in love; warm me, that my
love may go out to my neighbour.
I do not have a strong and firm
faith; at times I doubt and am
unable to trust you completely.
O Lord, help me.
Strengthen my faith and trust in you,
for your love's sake, Amen.

Martin Luther (adapted)

10th   **For discipleship**

Lord Jesus,
give me a tiny spark of your love, to
enable me to share in your work of
love. Let me always do first
whatever clear duty lies before me.

St Bernard of Clairvaux (adapted)

11th For knowledge of God

O God,
the light of the minds that know you,
the joy of the hearts that love you,
the strength of the wills that serve
you, help us so to know you that we
may truly love you; so to love you
that we may fully serve you, whom to
serve is perfect freedom, through
Jesus Christ our Lord, Amen.

St Augustine

12th For perseverance

Lord God,
when you give us work to do, help us
to remember that it is not the
beginning, but the continuing of the
same to the end, until it is
thoroughly finished, which manifests
your glory, through him who for the
finishing of your work laid down his
life, our Redeemer, Jesus Christ.

Sir Francis Drake (adapted)

13th In Christ's service

O Lord,
grant that we hold to you without
parting, worship you without
wearying, serve you without failing,
faithfully seek you, happily find
you, and for ever possess you, the
only God, now and for ever. Amen.

St Anselm

May

14th   Renewal in discipleship

O God,
renew our spirits with your Holy
Spirit, and draw our hearts to
yourself, that our work may not be a
burden but a delight. Let us not
serve as slaves with the spirit of
bondage, but with freedom and
gladness as your children, rejoicing
in your will, for Jesus Christ's
sake, Amen.

Benjamin Jenks

15th   For the gifts of the Holy Spirit

Come Holy Spirit, and daily increase
in us your gifts of grace; the
spirit of wisdom and understanding,
the spirit of counsel and strength,
the spirit of knowledge and true
godliness; and fill us with a spirit
of true reverence for you, now and
for evermore, Amen.

Gelasian Sacramentary (adapted)

16th   For new life in God's Spirit

O Lord Jesus Christ,
who on the first day of the week rose
again, raise up our souls to serve
the living God and daily renew and
enrich us with your Holy Spirit,
Amen.

Lancelot Andrewes (adapted)

17th   **For the faith of the newly baptised**

O God,
by whose spirit the whole body of the
Church is multiplied and governed;
preserve in the new-born children of
your family the fullness of your
grace; that being renewed in body
and soul, they may be fervent in the
faith, and be able to serve you
throughout their lives, through Jesus
Christ, Amen.

Gelasian Sacramentary

18th   **For Christian service**

Lord Jesus,
I give you my hands to do your work.
I give you my feet to go your way.
I give you my eyes to see as you do.
I give you my tongue to speak
your words.
I give you my mind that you may
think in me.
I give you my spirit that you may
pray in me.
Above all, I give you my heart that
you may love in me.

Lancelot Andrewes (abridged)

May

19th   For the Church in persecution

O God, our refuge and strength, our
very present help in trouble, have
mercy upon your Church in the midst
of oppression and persecution.
Deliver your people from tyranny and
wrong; keep them faithful in the
hour of trial and restore to them the
blessings of freedom and peace,
through Jesus Christ, Amen.

Unknown

20th   For all who minister

O Lord God Almighty,
who endowed your Apostles with gifts
of the Holy Spirit, give to all who
minister in your name the spirit of
wisdom and love, that in all their
words and deeds they may seek your
glory and increase your kingdom,
through Jesus Christ our Lord, Amen.

Adapted from an old Collect

21st **For faithfulness in God's service**

O God,
give us grace to do diligently and
patiently whatever duty you would
have us do. Go with us and we will
go. If you do not go with us, send
us not. If you send us out in your
service, go before us. Let us hear
your voice when we follow you.
Good Lord, hear our prayer.

Christina Rossetti (adapted)

22nd **For the spread of Christ's Kingdom**

O Merciful Father, whose blessed Son
was lifted up so as to draw all
people to him, take away from us all
that hinders the spread of your
kingdom.
Arouse the indifferent.
Lift up the fallen.
Strengthen the weak hearted.
Bring back wanderers.
Enlighten the ignorant and make the
Gospel of your Son known throughout
the world, for Jesus Christ's sake,
Amen.

L. Tuttiett (adapted)

May

23rd **The Christian Church**

Christ has no body now on earth but
ours, no hands but ours, no feet but
ours.
Ours are the eyes through which must
look out Christ's compassion on the
world. Ours are the feet with which
he is to go about doing good.
Ours are the hands with which he is
to bless us now.

St Teresa of Avila

24th **For unity**
O God, who loves all with an equal
love and calls us to worship you in
unity and peace, put away from us all
that causes us to differ, that with
your help we may keep the unity of
the Spirit in the bond of peace,
through Jesus Christ our Lord, Amen.

E. B. Pusey (adapted)

25th   **For unity in the Church**

O God, the Father of our Lord Jesus
Christ, our only Saviour, the Prince
of Peace,
give us grace seriously to lay to
heart the great dangers we are in by
our unhappy divisions.
Take away all hatred and prejudice
and all that hinders us from unity
and agreement.
Let us remember that as there is but
one Body and one Spirit, one hope of
our calling, one Lord, one Faith, one
Baptism, one God and Father of us
all, we may in future be all of one
heart and one soul, united in one
holy bond of truth and peace, of
faith and love, and may with one mind
and one voice glorify you, through
Jesus Christ our Lord, Amen.

Book of Common Prayer (adapted)

26th   **For the power of the Holy Spirit**

We beseech you, O God, let the power
of your Holy Spirit be present with
us, that our hearts may be cleansed
and we may be protected from all
adversities, through Jesus Christ our
Lord, Amen.

Leonine Sacramentary (adapted)

27th   **For Christ's salvation**

Remain, O Christ, in the hearts you
have redeemed.
You, who are perfect love, pour into
our words sincere repentance.
We raise our prayer to you, O Jesus.
Pardon the sin we have committed.
By the holy sign of the Cross, defend
us constantly as your children.

The Venerable Bede (adapted)

28th   **For zeal**

Almighty and most merciful Father,
make us with our whole heart to
hunger and thirst after you, and with
all our longing to desire you, for
the sake of your Son, our Saviour
Jesus Christ, to whom with you and
the Holy Spirit be all honour and
glory, for ever and ever, Amen.

St Anselm (abridged)

29th   **For endurance**

O God,
who has promised that they who endure
to the end shall be saved, give us
grace to persevere in your service
all our days, that we may reach the
end of our faith, even the salvation
of our soul, through Jesus Christ our
Lord, Amen.

The Narrow Way

30th   **For following Christ**

Lord Jesus,
who followed the way of suffering,
weakness and death before being
raised in glory, help us to follow
your way of love and to know that
suffering borne for your sake will
lead to your eternal glory, Amen.

P. N.

31st   **Glory to our ascended Lord**

Glory to our ascended Lord that he is
with us always.
Glory to him who has led captivity
captive and given gifts for the
perfecting of his saints.
Glory to him who has gone before us
to prepare a place in his Father's
home for us.
Glory to Jesus Christ, the author and
finisher of our faith, because
through him God is glorified.

Sursum Corda (abridged)

Jesus said, "Receive the Holy Spirit"
(John 20 : 22)

1st   **For receiving and sharing God's love**

Lord, make us instruments of
your peace.
Where there is hatred, let us
sow love.
Where there is injury, pardon.
Where there is discord, union.
Where there is doubt, faith.
Where there is despair, hope.
Where there is darkness, light.
Where there is sadness, joy.

For it is in giving that we receive.
It is in pardoning that we are
pardoned. It is in dying that we are
born to eternal life.

St Francis of Assisi

2nd   **For reverence of God**

Teach us, O God, to fear you without
being afraid; to fear you in love,
that we may love you without fear,
through Jesus Christ our Lord, Amen.

Christina Rossetti

3rd **For the gift of God's love**

O God,
who has taught us that all our doings
without love are worth nothing; send
your Holy Spirit, and pour into our
hearts that most excellent gift of
love, the very bond of peace. Give
this to us for the sake of Christ our
Saviour, Amen.

Thomas Cranmer (adapted)

4th **For God's love**

O God,
You know better than I how much I
love you. You know it and I know it
not, for nothing is more hidden from
me than the depths of my own heart.
I do want to love you. I fear I do
not love you enough.

François Fénelon (abridged)

5th **For illumination**

O God,
give us in the name of Jesus Christ
our Saviour, that love which can
never cease, that will kindle our
lamps but not extinguish them, that
they may burn in us and enlighten
others.

St Columba

June

6th   **For Christ's companionship**

O God our Father,
we come before you through the love
of your Son our Lord Jesus Christ and
ask you to fill our souls with love.
Be near to us day by day and hour by
hour, upholding us with your strength
and guiding us by your hand, until at
last you lead us home to your eternal
peace and joy, through the same Jesus
Christ our Lord, Amen.

Anonymous (adapted)

7th   **For God's blessing**

Bless us, O God our Father,
who created us.
Bless us, O God the Son,
who redeemed us.
Bless us, O God Holy Spirit,
who lives in us.
O Blessed Trinity keep us in body,
soul and spirit unto everlasting life.

Weimarischer Gesangbuch (adapted)

8th   **For Christ-likeness**

O Lord Jesus,
acknowledge what is yours in us, and
take away from us all that is not
yours, for the sake of your honour
and glory, Amen.

St Bernardine

9th   **On St Columba's Day**

Lord Christ,
Be thou a bright flame before me,
Be thou a guiding star above me,
Be thou a smooth path below me,
Today, tonight and for ever, Amen.

St Columba

10th   **For peace of mind**

O Lord,
calm the waves of this heart; calm
its tempest!
Calm yourself, O my soul, so that the
divine can act in you!
Calm yourself, O my soul, so that God
is able to repose in you, so that his
peace may cover you!

Søren Kierkegaard (abridged)

11th   **On St Barnabas' Day**

Lord Christ,
thank you for Barnabas, who loved and
served you, travelling to Antioch and
Cyprus with the good news of your
redeeming love.
Bless all those who teach and all who
learn, that together we may learn
knowledge of your ways and use it to
help the world, for your love's sake,
Amen.

P. N.

June

12th   **For Christ's Spirit**

O Saviour,
give to me your spirit of humility
and gentleness.
Annihilate all selfishness in me and
lead me into your way of universal
love and peace.

P. N.

13th   **For love of God and my neighbour**

My God,
I love you with my whole heart and
soul, and above all things, because
you are infinitely good and perfect
and most worthy of all my love.
And for your sake, I love my
neighbour as myself. Mercifully
grant, O my God, that having loved
you on earth, I may love and enjoy
you for ever in heaven.

Traditional Prayer

14th   **For receiving God's love**

Lord Jesus,
may the sweet burning ardour of your
love absorb my soul entirely and make
it a stranger to all that is not you
or for you, Amen.

St Francis of Assisi

15th   **For a heart filled with love**

Give me, O God, the most blessed gift
I know, a heart full of Christ's love,
Amen.

Co-workers of Mother Teresa

16th   **For God's Holy Spirit**

O Holy Spirit our comforter,
come today into our hearts and lead
our prayers to God our Father,
through Jesus Christ our Lord, Amen.

Mozarabic Liturgy (adapted)

17th   **For God's love**

Heavenly Father,
may I so love you and be loved by you
that I want to share that love with
all around me, and so find your peace
and joy in my heart.

P. N.

June

18th   **For Christian graces**

O God,
fill us with adoring gratitude to
you, for all that you are for us,
to us and in us. Fill us with love,
joy, peace and all the fruits of
your Spirit, through Jesus Christ
our Lord, Amen.

Christina Rossetti

19th   **For living by love**

O my God, let me walk in the way of love,
which knows not how to be selfish in
anything whatsoever.
Let me love you for yourself.
Let me love nothing instead of you.
Let your love work in me and by me,
and let me love you as you would be
loved by me.

Gertrude More (abridged)

20th   **Trusting in God's salvation**

God says, "I will save those who love me
and protect those who know me as Lord.
When they call to me,
I will answer them.
When they are in trouble,
I will be with them.
I will rescue them and honour them.
I will reward them with long life.
I will save them."

From Psalm 91

21st   **A hymn of praise**

How good it is to give thanks to you,
O Lord, to sing in your honour,
O Most High God; to proclaim your
constant love every morning and your
faithfulness every night.
Your mighty deeds, O Lord, make me
glad; because of what you have done,
I sing for joy.

From Psalm 92

22nd   **For love of God**

Most gracious God,
help me to love and seek you always
and everywhere, above all things and
for your sake, in this present life,
so that at length I may find you and
hold fast to you in the life to come,
Amen.

Archbishop Thomas Bradwardine
(adapted)

June

23rd   **For love and long-sufferance**

O holy and ever blessed God,
teach us to love one another,
to exercise forbearance and
forgiveness to our enemies,
never to return evil for evil,
but to be merciful as you, our Father
in Heaven, are merciful, Amen.

*New Church Book of Worship
(adapted)*

24th   **On the anniversary of the birth of
St John the Baptist**

Almighty God,
whose servant John the Baptist was
wonderfully born to fulfil your
purpose by preparing the way for the
advent of your Son:
lead us to repent according to his
preaching and after his example
constantly to speak the truth, boldly
rebuke vice and patiently suffer
for the truth's sake; through
Jesus Christ our Lord, Amen.

Alternative Service Book

25th   **For the gift of God's love**

O God, Fountain of Love,
give us your gift of love, that we
may love those whom you love with the
love that you give us, and so loving
our brothers and sisters for your
sake, may grow in love, and living in
love may live in you, for Jesus
Christ's sake, Amen.

E. B. Pusey (adapted)

26th   **For joy, peace and hope**

O God of Hope,
fill us, your children, with all joy
and peace in believing, that we may
abound in hope in the power of your
Holy Spirit, through Jesus Christ our
Lord, Amen.

Romans 15 : 13

27th   **For Christ's comfort and peace**

Lord Jesus,
As it seems good to you, give us
faith rather than knowledge, and hope
rather than assurance.
Feed us when we need feeding.
Heal us when we need healing.
Help us to find peace by lovingly
doing your good will.
Give us peace here and peace
hereafter, through Jesus Christ our
Lord, Amen.

Christina Rossetti (adapted)

June

28th   For knowledge of God

O God,
be present with us always and teach
us to come to you through your Son
our Lord Jesus Christ.
Keep us humble, gentle and wise to
know your will and to discern your
truth, for the sake of our Lord Jesus
Christ, Amen.

Dr Arnold (abridged and adapted)

29th   On St Peter's Day

Almighty God,
who inspired your apostle Saint Peter
to confess Jesus as Christ and Son of
the living God:
build up your Church upon this rock,
that in unity and peace it may
proclaim one truth and follow one
Lord, your Son our Saviour Jesus
Christ, Amen.

Alternative Service Book

30th   For God's peace

O God,
who is peace everlasting, whose
chosen reward is the gift of peace
and who has taught us that
peacemakers are your children,
pour your peace into our souls, that
everything discordant shall utterly
vanish, and all that makes for peace
be sweet to us for ever, through
Jesus Christ our Lord, Amen.

Mozarabic Prayer

Jesus said to his disciples, "if anyone wants to come with me, he must forget self, carry his cross, and follow me" (Matthew 16 : 24)

1st **For our rest in God**

Almighty God,
you have made us for yourself, so
that our hearts are restless until
they find their rest in you.
Give us purity of heart and strength
of purpose, so that no selfishness or
weakness on our part may prevent us
from doing your will, Amen.

St Augustine (adapted)

July

2nd   **In fear**

Lord God,
my heart is often afraid, fearful of
the future, old age, death,
misfortune, loss of loved ones,
failure, ill-will from others.

Forgive my lack of faith in you to
guide and protect me. Even if the
worst happens, you are always present
in it, so that the feared worst
cannot harm the eternal me.

Bishop George Appleton (adapted)

3rd   **For humility**

O God,
help us to think humbly of ourselves,
to consider our fellow human beings
with kindness, and to judge all they
say and do with the same
consideration and love which we
ourselves would like from them, Amen.

Jane Austen (adapted)

4th   **For reverence of life**

Eternal Father, source of life and
light, whose love extends to all
people, all creatures, all things:
grant us that reverence for life
which becomes those who believe in
you, lest we despise it, degrade it,
or come callously to destroy it.
Rather let us save it, secure it,
sanctify it, after the example of
your Son, Jesus Christ our Lord.

Archbishop Robert Runcie

5th　　　　**For surrender to God**

Take, Lord, all my liberty.
Receive my memory, my understanding
and my whole will. Whatever I have
and possess you have given me. To
you I restore it wholly, and to your
will I surrender it for your
direction. Help me to love you
before all else, Amen.

St Ignatius Loyala (adapted)

6th　　　　**For God's guidance**

O God,
govern everything by your wisdom, so
that my soul may always be serving
you in the way you will and not as
I choose.
Rid me of all selfishness, so that
I may serve you.
Let me live for you, who are life
itself, Amen.

St Teresa of Avila (adapted)

7th　　　　**For faithfulness**

Almighty God,
on whose love and support we entirely
depend, strengthen us with your
grace, so that even in the midst of
difficulty we shall continue to
follow the way of our Lord Jesus
Christ in faith and hope and love,
Amen.

P. N.

July

8th   **For justice**

Lord, give us faith that right makes might,
for the sake of all mankind, Amen.

Abraham Lincoln (adapted)

9th   **On St Thomas More's Day**

O God, giver of all good things,
give us a humble, quiet, peaceable,
patient, tender and loving mind.
May all our thoughts, words and deeds
be guided by your Holy Spirit.
These things, O God, that we pray
for, give us grace to work for, Amen.

St Thomas More
(abridged and adapted)

10th   **For service to God**

Heavenly Father,
help us to listen to your words,
to ask for your help,
to keep on doing your work and never
to stop loving our neighbours, for
your love's sake, Amen.

P. N.

11th   **For perseverance in work**

You, O God, sell us all good things
at the price of labour, Amen.

Leonardo da Vinci

12th   **To be needed**

O God,
give me work till my life shall end
and life till my work is done,
Amen.

Winifred Holtby

13th   **When we are too busy**

O God,
you know how busy I must be this day.
If I forget you, please do not forget
me.

Jacob Astley
(His battle prayer at Edgehill)

14th   **For patience**

O God,
help me to be more content with what
is present and less fearful about the
future. Give me patience in times of
loss and disappointment, for your
love's sake, Amen.

Bishop Simon Patrick (adapted)

July

15th   **For God's guidance**

May the strength of God pilot us.
May the power of God preserve us.
May the wisdom of God instruct us.
May the hand of God protect us.
May the way of God direct us.
May the shield of God defend us.
May the host of God guard us against
the snares of evil and the
temptations of the world.

Christ be with us.
Christ be before us.
Christ be in us.
Christ be over us.

St Patrick

16th   **For forgiveness**

Forgive us, O our Father,
for we have sinned.
Pardon us, O our King,
for we have transgressed.
Blessed are you, Eternal God, who
gives us your love and abundantly
pardons us.
Help us in our need and save us
quickly, for in you is our eternal
salvation.

Rabbi of Lissa (adapted)

17th **For increase of faith**

O Lord God,
in whom we live and move and have our
being, open our eyes that we may
discern your fatherly presence ever
with us. Draw our hearts to you with
the power of your love. Take from us
all doubt and distrust. Lift our
thoughts to you and make us know that
all things are possible to us through
your Son, our Saviour Jesus Christ,
Amen.

Bishop Brooke Foss Westcott
(abridged and adapted)

18th **For God's gift of grace**

O loving God, giver of grace, who
makes the poor in spirit rich in
virtue and makes the rich in goods
humble in heart!

O most Blessed grace, descend upon
me, refresh me early with your mercy
and your consolation that my soul may
not faint with weariness and dryness
of spirit.

I beg you, loving God, to fill me
with your grace, for even though
I may think I want more,
your grace is sufficient for me.

Thomas à Kempis (adapted)

July

19th   To work for God's glory

O God,
grant that I may do and suffer all
things this day for the glory of your
name, Amen.

Used by the Curé d'Ars

20th   When we feel we have no time

Lord,
I have time, plenty of time, all the
time you give me, the years of my
life, the days of my years, the hours
of my days, they are all mine —
mine to fill quietly, calmly, but to
fill completely up to the brim, to
offer them to you, that of their
insipid water you may make a rich
wine such as you made once in
Cana of Galilee.

I am not asking you tonight, Lord,
for time to do this and then that,
but your grace to do conscientiously,
in the time that you give me, what
you want me to do.

Michel Quoist (abridged)

21st   **For God's guidance**

O God,
never allow us to think that we can
manage on our own and not need you,
Amen.

John Donne

22nd   **On Mary Magdalen's Day**

Almighty God,
whose Son restored Mary Magdalen
to health of mind and body
and called her to be a witness
to his resurrection:
forgive us and heal us by your grace,
that we may serve you in the power of
his risen life; who is alive and
reigns with you and the Holy Spirit,
one God, now and for ever, Amen.

Alternative Service Book

July

23rd   **Petition to God**

O Lord our God,
our merciful Father in heaven,
give to us whatever is really good
and happy for us in soul and body,
and according to your will.
May we live as Christians, endure
with patience, and at the last die in
peace and hope, for Jesus Christ's
sake, Amen.

Johann Quirsfeld (adapted)

24th   **For renewal**

Almighty God,
make all things within us new
this day.
Renew our faith and hope and love.
Renew our wills that we may serve you
more gladly and watchfully than ever.
Renew our delight in your word and
your worship.
Renew our joy in you.
Renew our longing that all may
know you.
Renew our desires and labours to
serve others, and so take care of us,
your people, who embrace the Cross of
your Son and want to walk in the
light and power of your Spirit, now
and for always, through Jesus Christ
our Lord, Amen.

Unknown

25th   **On St Christopher's Day**

Lord Jesus,
thank you for all the help we receive
as we travel through life.
Help us to see you in those we meet,
and help others to see you in us.
Guide and protect us and bring us
safely home to our loved ones.
When our work is done and our journey
over, bring us to eternal rest with
you, Amen.

P. N.

26th   **For surrender to God's will**

O God,
make our service acceptable to you
while we live, and our souls ready
for you when we die, for the sake of
Jesus Christ, your Son, our Saviour,
Amen.

Archbishop Laud (adapted)

27th   **For strength**

Almighty God,
preserve us this day and strengthen
us to bear whatever you see fit to
give us, whether pain, sickness,
danger or distress, through Jesus
Christ our Lord, Amen.

Dr Arnold

July

28th   **For protection**

O God,
who orders all things, both in heaven
and on earth, put away from us all
hurtful things and give us only those
things which are profitable to us,
through Jesus Christ our Lord, Amen.

Book of Common Prayer (adapted)

29th   **For joy and peace today**

O God, Holy Spirit within us,
help us to pass this day in gladness
and peace, without stumbling and
without stain, Amen.

Mozarabic Prayer (abridged)

30th   **Commendation**

Into your hands, Almighty God,
we commend our souls and bodies for
your most mighty protection.
Strengthen us for your service this
day, through Jesus Christ our Lord,
Amen.

Archbishop Laud

31st   **For serving God**

Teach us, good Lord, to serve thee as
thou deservest:
to give and not to count the cost,
to fight and not to heed the wounds,
to toil and not to seek for rest,
to labour and not to ask for any
reward, save that of knowing that we
do thy will, Amen.

St Ignatius Loyola

Let us run with determination the race
that lies before us. Let us keep our eyes
fixed on Jesus, on whom our faith depends
from beginning to end.   (Hebrews 12 : 1, 2)

1st   **For guidance**

O God, I know not what I ought to ask
of you.
You alone know what I need.
You love me better than I know how to
love myself.
O Father, give to your child that for
which I know not how to ask.
I want to want only to do your will.
Teach me to pray.
Pray yourself in me.

François Fénelon
(abridged and adapted)

2nd   **For understanding God's love**

O Father,
help us to know that the hiding of
your face from us is wise love.
Your love is not doting and
reasonless. Your children must often
have the frosty, cold side of the
hill, and set down both their bare
feet among the thorns.
Your love has eyes, and in the
meantime is looking on.
Our pride must have winter weather.
O Father, help us to know your love
is wise love, Amen.

George MacDonald (adapted)

3rd   **For silence**

Saviour,
teach me the silence of humility,
the silence of wisdom,
the silence of love,
the silence of perfection,
the silence that speaks without words,
the silence of faith.
Lord,
teach me to silence my own heart that
I may listen to the gentle movement
of the Holy Spirit within me and
sense the depths which are of God.

Traditional German prayer

August

4th   **For freedom**

O God,
who has taught us that we are most
truly free when we find our wills in
yours; help us to gain this liberty
by continual surrender to you, that
we may walk in the way you have
planned for us, and in doing your
will we may find our life.

Gelasian Sacramentary

5th   **For freedom in Christ**

O Lord my God, I hope in thee.
My dear Lord Jesus, set me free.
In chains, in pains,
I long for thee.
On bended knee
I adore thee, implore thee
to set me free.

Mary Queen of Scots

6th   **For perseverance**

O God,
who commanded that no one should be
idle, help us to use all our talents
and faculties in the work you have
appointed us to do, for your love's
sake, Amen.

James Martineau (adapted)

7th   **For an open mind**

O God,
Help us not to despise or oppose what
we do not understand, Amen.

William Penn

8th　　**For the guidance of God**

Strengthen me, O God, by the grace of
your Holy Spirit. Let me be so
strengthened inwardly that I may put
away all useless anxiety and
distress.

Thomas à Kempis
(abridged and adapted)

9th　　**For endurance**

O God,
give me a steadfast heart, which
nothing unworthy may drag downwards.
Give me an unconquered heart, which
no tribulation can wear out.
Give me an upright heart, which no
unworthy purpose may tempt aside.

Thomas Aquinas (adapted)

10th　　**For seeking God's presence**

O God, who is all wisdom,
give me understanding to know you,
diligence to seek you, wisdom to find
you and a faithfulness that may
finally embrace you.

Thomas Aquinas

August

11th   **For guidance**

We beg you, O Lord our God, that in
whatever dangers we are placed we may
call upon your name, and that when
you have delivered us we may never
cease from praising you, through
Christ our Lord, Amen.

Leonine Sacramentary (adapted)

12th   **For patience in trial**

O God,
do not permit my trials to be above
my strength and be my comfort and
strength in time of trial.
Give me grace to take in good part
whatever happens to me, and let my
heart acknowledge it to be permitted
by your providence.

Thomas Wilson (adapted)

13th   **Prayer for help**

From the depths of my despair, I call
to you, Lord. Hear my cry, O Lord.
Listen to my call for help. If you
kept a record of our sins, who could
escape being condemned? But you
forgive us, so that we should stand
in awe of you.
I wait eagerly for the Lord's help
and in his word I trust. I wait for
the Lord more eagerly than watchmen
wait for the dawn, than watchmen wait
for the dawn.

From Psalm 130

14th   **For help from God**

O God, helper of the helpless,
be within me to strengthen me.
Be above me to protect me.
Be beneath me to uphold me.
Be before me to direct me.
Be behind me to keep me from
straying.
Be round about me to defend me.
Blessed are you, O God our Father,
for ever and ever, Amen.

Lancelot Andrewes
(abridged and adapted)

15th   **For guidance**

Almighty God,
teach us to do your will, that we may
inwardly love you before all else and
with a pure mind. For you are our
Maker and Redeemer, our Help and
Comfort, our Trust and our Hope.
Praise and glory be to you now and
for ever, Amen.

King Alfred (adapted)

August

16th   **For God's protection**

O Father in heaven,
guide us through the darkness of this
world. Guard us from its perils and
strengthen us when we grow weary.
Lead us by your chosen paths through
time and through death to our eternal
home in your heavenly kingdom. We
ask this in the name of Jesus Christ
our Lord, Amen.

Old liturgy (adapted)

17th   **In temptation**

O loving God, our Protector,
arm us with your grace and assist us
with your Holy Spirit in all kinds of
temptations, through Jesus Christ our
Lord, Amen.

Archbishop Grindal (abridged)

18th   **For God's protection**

O God,
our most mighty and loving Protector,
guard us in peril. Direct us in
doubt and save us from falling into
sin. Deliver us from the evil that
is around and within us. Make the
path of our duty plain to us and keep
us in it to the end, through Jesus
Christ our Lord, Amen.

Old liturgy (adapted)

19th   **For perseverance**

O God, the might of all who put their
trust in you, help us to conquer all
that makes war upon our souls and in
the end to enter into your perfect
peace and presence, through Jesus
Christ our Lord, Amen.

Roman Breviary

20th   **For Christ's companionship**

O Lord God,
be with our spirit and live in our
hearts by faith. Be with us
everywhere and at all times and in
all the circumstances of our life, to
bless and help us.
Never leave us, till you have brought
us through all trials and dangers to
be for ever with you, Amen.

Benjamin Jenks (abridged)

21st   **For enlightenment**

O heavenly Father,
the author and fountain of truth,
the bottomless sea of all
understanding, send your Holy Spirit
into our hearts and lighten our
understandings with the beams of your
heavenly grace. We ask this,
O merciful Father, for the sake of
your dear Son, our Lord Jesus Christ,
Amen.

Bishop Nicholas Ridley

August

22nd   **For guidance**

Be merciful to me, Lord, for I am in
trouble; my eyes are tired from so
much crying; I am completely worn
out. I am exhausted by sorrow and
weeping has shortened my life. I am
weak from all my troubles; even my
bones are wasting away.
But my trust is in you, O Lord. You
are my God. I am always in your
care; save me from my enemies, from
those who persecute me.

From Psalm 31

23rd   **Longing for God**

As a deer longs for a stream of cool
water, so I long for you, O God.
I thirst for you, the living God.
When can I go and worship in your
presence? Day and night I cry, and
tears are my only food. All the time
my enemies ask me, 'Where is your
God?'
Why am I so sad? Why am I so
troubled?
I will put my hope in God and once
again I will praise him, my saviour
and my God.

From Psalm 42

24th   **Prayer for help**

Be merciful to me, O God, be
merciful, because I come to you for
safety. In the shadow of your wings
I find protection until the raging
storms are over.
I call to God, the Most High;
to God, who supplies my every need.
He will answer from heaven and save
me. He will defeat my oppressors.
God will show me his constant love
and faithfulness. I have complete
confidence, O God; I will sing and
praise you.

From Psalm 57

25th   **Prayer from a troubled heart**

Listen to my prayer, O Lord, and hear
my cry for help. When I am in
trouble, don't turn away from me.
Listen to me and answer me quickly
when I call.
The Lord has made me weak while I am
still young. He has shortened my
life. O God, do not take me away now
before I grow old.

From Psalm 102

August

26th   **For personal guidance**

Be good to me, your servant, so that
I may live and obey your teachings.
Open my eyes, so that I may see the
wonderful truths in your law. I am
here on earth for just a little
while; do not hide your commands
from me. My heart aches with
longing; I want to know your
judgements at all times.

From Psalm 119

27th   **Prayer for help**

Let my cry for help reach you, Lord.
Give me understanding, as you have
promised. Listen to my prayer, and
save me according to your promise.
I will always praise you, because you
teach me your laws. How I long for
your saving help, O Lord.

From Psalm 119

28th   **For help from God**

O God our Father, hear me, who am
trembling in this darkness and
stretch out your arms to me. Hold
your light before me and be my guide,
so I may be restored to myself and to
you.

St Augustine (adapted)

29th　　**On St John the Baptist's Day**

O God, our Father,
we thank you for the courage and love
of John the Baptist in preparing the
way for your coming into the world
through our Lord Jesus Christ.

Give us also courage to proclaim our
faith in you and so help prepare the
hearts of others to receive you, for
your love's sake, Amen.

P. N.

30th　　**Prayer for help**

I call to the Lord for help.
I plead with him.
I bring him all my complaints.
I tell him all my troubles.
When I am ready to give up, he knows
what I should do.
Lord, I cry to you for help.
You, Lord, are my protector.

From Psalm 142

31st　　**For light and truth**

O God,
may your Spirit illuminate our minds
and lead us into all truth, through
Jesus Christ our Lord, Amen.

Gelasian Sacramentary (adapted)

SEPTEMBER

In the name of our Lord Jesus Christ, always give thanks for everything to God the Father. (Ephesians 5 : 20)

1st   **Thanksgiving**

O God,
you have given so much to me;
give me one thing more,
a grateful heart.

George Herbert

2nd   **Thanksgiving**

Thanks be to you, O God,
my joy, my hope and my glory.
Thanks be to you for your gifts
to me.
Thanks be to you for your gift
of my life.
Preserve and strengthen your
life in me.

St Augustine (adapted)

3rd   **For gratitude to God**

And still, O God, to me impart
an innocent and grateful heart.

Samuel Taylor Coleridge

September

4th   **Thanksgiving to God**

I will praise you, Lord, with all
my heart.
I will tell of all the wonderful
things you have done.
I will sing with joy because of you.
I will sing praise to you,
Almighty God.

The Lord is a refuge for the
oppressed, a place of safety in times
of trouble.
Those who know you, Lord, will
trust you.
You do not abandon anyone who
comes to you.

From Psalm 9

5th   **General Thanksgiving**

Almighty God, Creator and Redeemer,
thank you for the gift of life and
the means of sustaining it.
Thank you for beauty and variety in
creation.
Thank you for my own personal
blessings and for your gift of love
and forgiveness in Jesus Christ our
Lord.
Thank you for being with me now and
in eternity. Help me to receive you
and stay close to you all my life,
Amen.

P. N.

6th   **Safe with God**

Alone with none but Thee, my God,
I journey on my way.
What need I fear when Thou art near,
Oh King of night and day?
More safe am I within thy hand
Than if a host did round me stand.

Attributed to St Columba

7th   **Praise to God in Trinity**

Praise and glory be to the
omnipotence of God, Eternal Father,
who in his providence created the
world out of nothing.
Praise and glory be to the wisdom of
God, the only-begotten Son, who
redeemed the world with his life.
Praise and glory be to the loving
kindness of God, Holy Spirit, who
enlightens the world in faith.
Praise and glory be to you, O God,
Father, Son and Holy Spirit,
undivided Trinity, who formed us in
your own image, Amen.

Latin, 11th century (adapted)

September

8th   **For knowledge of God's love**

The sun is shining . . .
thank you Lord.
I mean it is shining: the sky and
everything is warm and smiling.
But it is not only that . . .
my heart is smiling.
I know that I am loved . . .
and that I love too.
Thank you, Lord, the sun is shining.

Michael Hollings and Etta Gullick

9th   **Thanksgiving to God**

O God,
as truly as you are our father, so
just as truly are you our mother.
We thank you God, our father, for
your strength and goodness.
We thank you God, our mother, for the
closeness of your caring.
O God, our loving parent,
we thank you for the great love you
have for each one of us, Amen.

Julian of Norwich (adapted)

10th   **For the gift of sight**

O Lord God,
who has given me the gift of sight,
help me to see not only with the eyes
of my head but with the eyes of the
heart also, that I may perceive the
beauty and meaning of all I see, and
glorify you, the Creator of all, for
your love's sake, Amen.

Bishop George Appleton

11th   **Thanksgiving for God's love**

O God,
we give thanks to you for sending
your only Son to die for us all.
In a world divided by class and race
and creed, how sweet it is to know
that in you we all belong to one
family.

*A Bantu pastor
(abridged and adapted)*

12th   **For joy**

O God,
I thank you for all the joy I have
had in life.

Earl Brihtnoth

13th **For giving thanks at all times**

O God, our strength and stay,
help us to pray always and not to
faint. In everything, help us to
give thanks, offering up the
sacrifice of praise continually,
possessing our souls in patience, and
learning in all circumstances to be
content, for the sake of Jesus
Christ, our Lord and Master, Amen.

Fielding Ould

14th **Thanks for liberty in Christ Jesus**

O God,
we thank you for freedom of worship,
of thought and of speech.
Let our religion not divide us from
others, but draw us together in
fellowship and love.

Francis W. Newman (adapted)

15th **Thanksgiving for prayer**

O Christ, our friend and master,
we thank you for teaching us how to
pray simply and sincerely to you, and
for hearing us when we call to you.
We thank you for saving us from our
sins and sorrows, and for directing
all our ways this day. Lead us ever
onwards to yourself, for your love's
sake, Amen.

Father John of Russia (adapted)

16th **Thanksgiving for our redemption**

Glory be to God in the highest, the
Creator, the Lord of heaven and
earth, the Preserver of all things,
the Father of mercies, who so loved
mankind as to send his only begotten
Son into the world, to redeem us from
sin and misery and to obtain for us
everlasting life.
Accept, O gracious God, our praises
and our thanksgivings for your
infinite mercies towards us. Teach
us, O God, to love you more and serve
you better, through Jesus Christ our
Lord, Amen.

Bishop Hamilton

17th **Thanksgiving for our eternal life**

O God our loving father,
we thank you for all the joy of our
humanity, but chiefly for the joy of
sin forgiven, weakness strengthened,
victory promised and the hope of life
eternal, through Jesus Christ our
Lord, Amen.

George Dawson
(abridged and adapted)

18th   **Thanksgiving for the harvest**

O Almighty God and Heavenly Father,
we thank you that you have again
fulfilled your promise of an annual
seed-time and harvest.
Help us to remember also that it is
not by bread alone that we live.
Help us to be sustained by him, who
is the true bread from heaven, Jesus
Christ our Lord, to whom with you,
Father, and your Holy Spirit, be all
honour and glory, world without end,
Amen.

Church of Ireland prayer (adapted)

19th   **God's grace in answering prayer**

I pray to you, O God, because you
answer me; so turn to me and listen
to my words.
Reveal your wonderful love and save
me; at your side I am safe from
my enemies.
Glory be to the Father and to the Son
and the Holy Spirit, as it was in the
beginning is now and ever shall be,
world without end, Amen.

From Psalm 17

20th   **Thanksgiving**

Heavenly Father,
make us thankful to you and
thoughtful for others as we receive
your blessings, in Jesus' name, Amen.

Book of Common Worship

21st   **On St Matthew's Day**

Almighty God,
who through your Son Jesus Christ
called Matthew from the selfish
pursuit of gain to become an apostle
and evangelist:
free us from all possessiveness and
love of riches that we may follow in
the steps of Jesus Christ our Lord;
who is alive and reigns with you and
the Holy Spirit, one God, now and for
ever, Amen.

Alternative Service Book

22nd   **Thanks for the bright things of life**

O God,
we would thank you for all the bright
things of life. Help us to see them
and to count them and to remember
them, that our lives may be given to
you in praise, for the sake of Jesus
Christ our Lord, Amen.

J. H. Jowett (adapted)

23rd   **Thanks for God's goodness**

How precious, O God, is your
constant love!
We find protection under the shadow
of your wings.
We feast on the abundant food you
provide;
you let us drink from the river of
your goodness.
You are the source of all life, and
because of your light we see the
light.

From Psalm 36

24th   **Desire to obey God**

O God,
your teachings are wonderful;
I obey them with all my heart.
The explanation of your teachings
gives light and brings wisdom to the
ignorant.
As you have promised, keep me from
falling;
don't let me be overcome by evil.
Save me from those who oppress me, so
that I may obey your commands.
Bless me with your presence and teach
me your laws.
My tears pour down like a river,
because people do not obey your law.

From Psalm 119

25th   **Prayer for help**

I have complete confidence, O God!
I will sing and praise you!
Wake up, my soul!
Wake up, my harp and lyre!
I will wake up the sun.
I will thank you, O Lord, among
the nations.
I will praise you among the peoples.
Your constant love reaches among
the heavens;
your faithfulness touches the skies.
Show your greatness in the sky,
O God, and your glory over all
the earth.
Save us by your might; answer my
prayer, so that the people you love
may be rescued, Amen.

From Psalm 108

26th   **A prayer of thanksgiving**

Give thanks to the Lord, because he
is good; his love is eternal.
Give thanks to the greatest of all
gods; his love is eternal.
Give thanks to the mightiest of all
lords; his love is eternal.

He alone performs great miracles;
his love is eternal.
By his wisdom he made the heavens;
his love is eternal.
He built the earth on the deep
waters; his love is eternal.
He made the sun and moon;
his love is eternal;
the sun to rule over the day;
his love is eternal;
the moon and the stars to rule over
the night; his love is eternal.
Give thanks to the God of heaven;
his love is eternal.

From Psalm 136

27th   **Thanksgiving for life and work**

Almighty and merciful God,
we give you thanks for the light of
another day, for the work we have to
do and the strength to do it.
We pray that you should guide us by
your truth, uphold us by your power
and purify us by the continual
indwelling of your Spirit.
Help us to grow in wisdom, to know
the things that belong to our peace
and give us the strength to persevere
until the end, through Jesus Christ
our Lord, Amen.

Dean Goulbourn

28th   **For saintliness**

Lord,
make me a saint according to your own
heart – meek and humble, for Jesus
Christ's sake, Amen.

Mother Teresa of Calcutta

29th   **Thanksgiving for the saints**

We thank you, O God, for the saints
of all ages: for those who in times
of darkness kept the lamp of faith
burning; for the great souls who saw
visions of larger truth and dared to

declare it; for the multitude of
quiet and gracious souls whose
presence has purified and sanctified
the world; and for those known and
loved by us, who have passed from
this earthly fellowship into fuller
life with you, Amen.

Anonymous

30th   **Thanksgiving for everything**

'Night is drawing nigh –'
For all that has been – Thanks!
To all that shall be – Yes!

Dag Hammarskjöld

OCTOBER

'I pray that they may all be one, Father!
May they be in us just as you are in me
and I am in you. May they be one, so that
the world will believe that you sent me'.
(John 17 : 21)

1st   **For fellowship in Christ**

O God,
Dispose us to give one another the
kiss of peace, since we have been
called to one hope in Jesus Christ,
Amen.

St Basil the Great

2nd   **Praise**

O God,
I will sing about your strength;
every morning I will sing aloud of
your constant love.
You have been a refuge for me,
a shelter in time of trouble.
I will praise you, my defender.
My refuge is God,
the God who loves me.

From Psalm 59

3rd   **For eternal blessing**

O God,
may we, who have been given reason
and speech, always bless you with our
heart and lips and may we inherit
your blessing, even the eternal
blessedness of heaven, Amen.

Christina Rossetti (adapted)

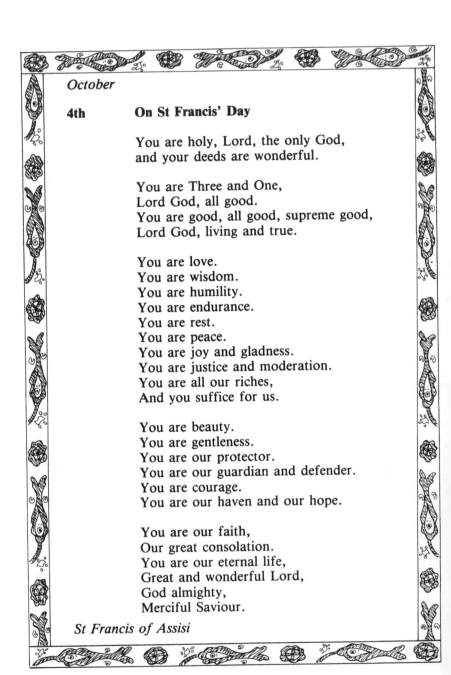

October

4th　　**On St Francis' Day**

You are holy, Lord, the only God,
and your deeds are wonderful.

You are Three and One,
Lord God, all good.
You are good, all good, supreme good,
Lord God, living and true.

You are love.
You are wisdom.
You are humility.
You are endurance.
You are rest.
You are peace.
You are joy and gladness.
You are justice and moderation.
You are all our riches,
And you suffice for us.

You are beauty.
You are gentleness.
You are our protector.
You are our guardian and defender.
You are courage.
You are our haven and our hope.

You are our faith,
Our great consolation.
You are our eternal life,
Great and wonderful Lord,
God almighty,
Merciful Saviour.

St Francis of Assisi

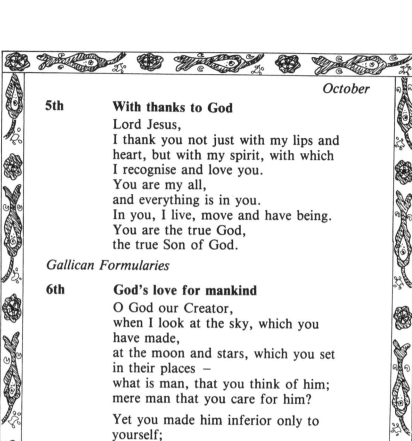

5th   **With thanks to God**

Lord Jesus,
I thank you not just with my lips and
heart, but with my spirit, with which
I recognise and love you.
You are my all,
and everything is in you.
In you, I live, move and have being.
You are the true God,
the true Son of God.

Gallican Formularies

6th   **God's love for mankind**

O God our Creator,
when I look at the sky, which you
have made,
at the moon and stars, which you set
in their places –
what is man, that you think of him;
mere man that you care for him?

Yet you made him inferior only to
yourself;
you crowned him with glory and
honour.
You appointed him ruler over
everything you made;
you placed him over all creation;
sheep and cattle, and the wild
animals too;
the birds and the fish
and the creatures of the sea.

O Lord, our Lord,
your greatness is seen in all the
world!

From Psalm 8

7th **Our response to God**

All you that are righteous,
shout for joy for what the Lord
has done;
praise him, all you that obey him.
Give thanks to the Lord with harps,
sing to him with stringed
instruments.
Sing a new song to him, play the harp
with skill, and shout for joy!

The words of the Lord are true
and all his works are dependable.
The Lord loves what is righteous
and just;
his constant love fills the earth,
Amen.

From Psalm 33

8th **In praise of God**

O God,
the day is yours
and the night is yours;
you have prepared the light
and the sun;
they continue this day according to
your ordinance,
for all things serve you.
Praise be to you, O God, who turns
the shadow of death into the morning,
and renews the face of the earth.

Lancelot Andrewes (adapted)

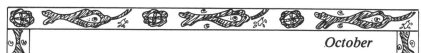

9th   **The harvest of prayer**

I asked for strength that I might achieve. I was made weak that I might learn humbly to obey.

I asked for health that I might do greater things. I was given infirmity that I might do better things.

I asked for riches that I might be happy. I was given poverty that I might be wise.

I asked for power that I might have the praise of men. I was given weakness that I might feel the need of God.

I asked for all things that I might enjoy life. I was given life that I might enjoy all things.

I got nothing that I asked for, but everything that I had hoped for.

Almost despite myself, my unspoken prayers were answered. I am, among all people, most richly blessed.

Prayer of an unknown confederate soldier

10th   **For joy**

O God our Creator,
as the hand is made for holding and
the eye for seeing, you have
fashioned me for joy.

Share with me the vision that shall
find it everywhere:
    in the wild violet's beauty;
    in the lark's melody;
    in the face of a steadfast man;
    in a child's smile;
    in a mother's love;
    in the purity of Jesus, Amen.

Gaelic

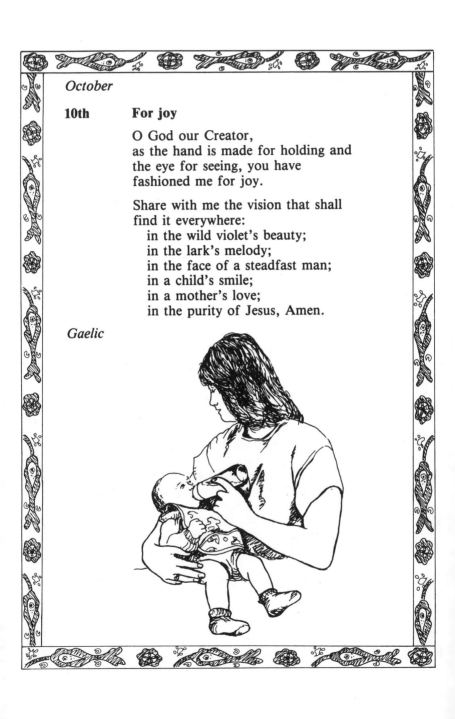

11th   **Adoration**

O burning mountain,
O chosen sun,
O perfect moon,
O fathomless well,
O unattainable height,
O clearness beyond measure,
O wisdom without end,
O mercy without limit,
O strength beyond resistance,
O crown of all majesty,
The humblest you created sings your
praise.

Mechtild of Magdeburg

12th   **In praise of God**

What else can I do, a lame old man,
but sing hymns to God?
If I were a nightingale, I would do
the nightingale's part.
If I were a swan, I would do as a swan.
But now I am a rational creature, and
I ought to praise God: this is my
work; I do it, nor will I desert my
post, so long as I am allowed to keep
it. And I exhort you to join me in
the same song.

Epictetus

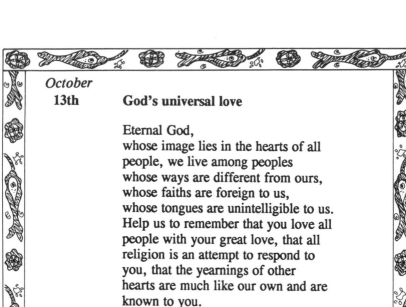

October

13th   **God's universal love**

Eternal God,
whose image lies in the hearts of all
people, we live among peoples
whose ways are different from ours,
whose faiths are foreign to us,
whose tongues are unintelligible to us.
Help us to remember that you love all
people with your great love, that all
religion is an attempt to respond to
you, that the yearnings of other
hearts are much like our own and are
known to you.
Help us to recognise you in the words
of truth, the things of beauty and
the actions of love about us.
We pray through Christ, who is a
stranger to no one land more than
another, and to every land no less
than to another.

World Council of Churches

14th   **In praise of God**

Let all the world in every corner sing,
My God and King!
The Church with psalms must shout,
No door can keep them out;
But above all the heart
Must bear the longest part.
Let all the world in every corner sing,
My God and King!

George Herbert (abridged)

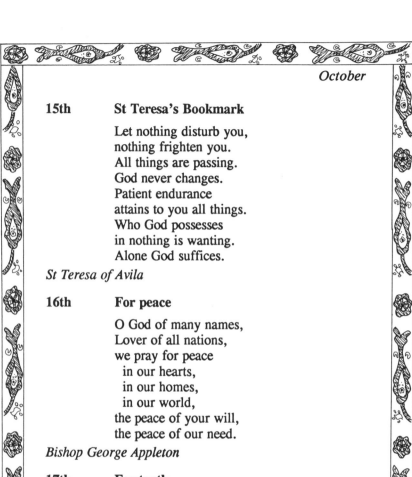

15th **St Teresa's Bookmark**

Let nothing disturb you,
nothing frighten you.
All things are passing.
God never changes.
Patient endurance
attains to you all things.
Who God possesses
in nothing is wanting.
Alone God suffices.

St Teresa of Avila

16th **For peace**

O God of many names,
Lover of all nations,
we pray for peace
  in our hearts,
  in our homes,
  in our world,
the peace of your will,
the peace of our need.

Bishop George Appleton

17th **For truth**

From the cowardice
that shrinks from truth,
From the laziness
that is content with half-truth,
From the arrogance
that thinks it knows all truth,
O God of Truth deliver us.

Ancient collect

October

18th   **On St Luke's Day**

Almighty God,
who inspired Luke the physician to
proclaim the love and healing power
of your Son: give your Church, by the
grace of the Spirit and through the
medicine of the Gospel, the same love
and power to heal; through Jesus
Christ our Lord, Amen.

Alternative Service Book

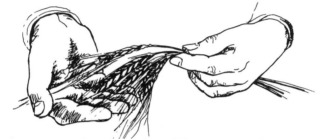

19th   **Adoration of our Creator**

We worship and adore the framer and
former of the universe:
governor, disposer, keeper;
Him on whom all things depend;
mind and spirit of the world;
from whom all things spring;
by whose spirit we live;
the divine spirit diffused through all;
God all-powerful;
God always present;
God above all other gods;
Thee we worship and adore.

Seneca

20th   **At peace**

Almighty One,
in the woods I am blessed.
Happy everyone in the woods.
Every tree speaks through thee.
O God, what glory in the woodland!
On the heights is peace -
peace to serve Him.

Beethoven

21st   **In praise of God**

Fill thou my life, O Lord my God,
in every part with praise,
that my whole being may proclaim
thy being and thy ways.

So shall no part of day or night
unblest or common be;
But all my life, in every step,
be fellowship with thee.

H. Bonar (abridged)

22nd   **For God's presence**

My God, my God, let me for once look on thee
as though nought else existed, we alone!
And as creation crumbles, my soul's spark
expands till I can say - even for myself,
I need thee and I feel thee and I love thee.

Robert Browning

October

23rd   **For blessing**

May the road rise to meet us.
May the wind be always at our backs.
May the sun shine warm upon our faces.
May the rain fall softly upon our
fields until we meet again.
May God hold us in the hollow of his
hands.

Old Gaelic Prayer

24th   **For unity**

O God of peace,
good beyond all that is good, in whom
is calmness and concord:
Make up the dissensions which divide
us from one another, and bring us
into unity of love in you; through
Jesus Christ our Lord, Amen.

Liturgy of St Dionysius (adapted)

25th   **For a good end to life**

O God,
giver of all good things.
grant me a good end –
what is above every gift –
a good and holy end to life,
a glorious and joyful resurrection.

Lancelot Andrewes (abridged)

26th   **For praise of God in music**

Praise the Lord!
Praise God in his Temple!
Praise his strength in heaven!
Praise him for the mighty things he
has done.
Praise his excellent greatness.
Praise him with trumpets.
Praise him with harps and lyres.
Praise him with cymbals and dancing.
Praise him with strings and flutes.
Praise him with well-tuned cymbals
and loud drums.
Let everything that has breath,
Praise the Lord!

Psalm 150 (adapted)

October

27th   **Glory to God**

Almighty God,
whose glory the heavens are telling,
the earth your power and the sea your
might, to you belong glory, honour,
might, greatness and magnificence,
now and for ever, to the ages of
ages, through Jesus Christ our Lord,
Amen.

Liturgy of St James (adapted)

28th   **Blessing to God in Trinity**

Blessing and honour, thanksgiving and
praise, more than we can utter, be
unto thee, O most adorable Trinity,
Father, Son and Holy Spirit, by all
angels, all people, all creatures, for
ever and ever, Amen.

Bishop Thomas Ken (adapted)

29th   **For God's peace**

Deep peace of the Running Wave,
Deep peace of the Flowing Air,
Deep peace of the Quiet Earth,
Deep peace of the Shining Stars,
Deep peace of the Son of Peace
Be with us now and always, Amen.

Old Celtic Blessing

30th   **For God's blessing**

O God,
grant that we may live in your fear,
die in your favour, rest in your
peace, rise in your power and reign
in your glory, for your beloved Son's
sake, Jesus Christ our Lord, Amen.

Archbishop Laud

31st   **For God's eternal blessing**

O God,
let your fatherly hand ever be over us;
let your Holy Spirit ever be
with us and so lead us in the
knowledge and obedience of your word,
that at the end we may obtain eternal
life, through Jesus Christ our Lord,
Amen.

Archbishop Hermann

Turn away from your sins, because the
Kingdom of heaven is near! (Matthew 3 : 2)

1st   **On All Saints Day**

O Lord our God,
from whom neither life nor death can
separate those who trust in your
love, and whose love holds in its
embrace your children in this world
and the next; so unite us in
yourself that in fellowship with you
we may always be united to our loved
ones whether here or there.
Give us courage, constancy and hope,
through him who died and was buried
and rose again for us, Jesus Christ
our Lord, Amen.

Archbishop Temple

2nd   **On All Souls Day**

Heavenly Father,
into whose hands your Son, our Lord
Jesus Christ, commended his spirit at
his last hour, into those same hands
we commend all those in our hearts
today. May they find eternal
fellowship with you.

P. N.

3rd   **Confession**

Almighty God, our heavenly Father,
we have sinned against you and
against our fellow human beings,
in thought and word and deed,
through negligence, through weakness,
through our own deliberate fault.

We are truly sorry
and repent of all our sins.
For the sake of your Son Jesus Christ,
who died for us,
forgive us all that is past;
and grant that we may serve you
in newness of life;
to the glory of your name, Amen.

Alternative Service Book

4th **For receiving Christ worthily**

O God,
let the remembrance of all the glory
wherein I was created make me more
serious and humble, more deep and
penitent, more pure and holy before
thee.

Thomas Traherne

5th **Prayer for help**

Answer me when I pray,
O God, my defender.
When I was in trouble, you helped me.
Be kind to me now and hear my prayer.

From Psalm 4

6th **For insight**

Lord,
give me an open heart to find you
everywhere, to glimpse the heaven
enfolded in a bud and experience
eternity in the smallest act of love.

Friend of Mother Teresa

November

7th   **Prayer for protection**

Listen to my words, O Lord,
and hear my sighs.
Listen to my cry for help,
my God and king.
I pray to you, O Lord;
you hear my voice in the morning;
at sunrise I offer my prayer
and wait for your answer.
Lead me to do your will;
make your way plain for me to follow.

From Psalm 5

8th   **Adoration**

Come, my Light, and illumine my
darkness.
Come, my Life, and revive me from
death.
Come, my Physician, and heal my
wounds.
Come, Flame of divine love, and burn
up the thorns of my sins, kindling my
heart with the flame of your love.
Come, my King, sit upon the throne of
my heart and reign there, for you
alone are my King and Lord.

St Dimitrii of Rostov

9th   **In sorrow for my sins**

Make me a clean heart, O God, and
renew a right spirit within me. Cast
me not away from your presence and
take not your Holy Spirit from me.

From Psalm 51

10th   **In penitence**

O God,
who forgives all who are penitent,
forgive me:
the wrong of ignorance,
the wrong of thoughtlessness,
the wrong of not having followed you
with a melting heart,
the wrong of not having meditated
upon you,
the wrong of not having prayed and
worshipped you,
O Supreme Almighty, forgive me of
all, all my wrongs.

Pattinatar

November

11th　　**On Armistice Day**

Almighty God,
May the memory of two world wars
strengthen our efforts for peace.
May the memory of those who died
inspire our service to the living.
May the memory of past destruction
move us to build for the future.
O God of peace,
O Father of souls,
O Builder of the Kingdom of Love,
Amen.

Bishop George Appleton

12th　　**For God's guidance**

O God, my Guide and Redeemer,
help me to know what I ought to know,
to love what I ought to love,
to praise what delights you most,
to value what is precious in your
sight and to hate what is offensive
to you, Amen.

Thomas à Kempis (abridged)

13th　　**For God's guidance**

Speak, Lord, for your servant is
listening.
Give us ears to hear, eyes to see,
wills to obey and hearts to love.
Then declare what you will,
reveal what you will, command what
you will and demand what you will,
for Christ's sake, Amen.

Christina Rossetti

14th **For purified lives**

O God,
in your mercy, give to us the fire of
your love, so as to burn up all
things in us which are displeasing
to you.
Make us ready for your heavenly
kingdom, for the sake of Jesus Christ
our Saviour, Amen.

Roman Breviary

15th **For humility and repentance**

O merciful God,
take away from my heart all self-
pride and boasting, all desire to
excuse myself for my sins or wish to
blame others for my faults. Rather,
let me take as my example and guide
him who chose to be crowned with
thorns and die for us all, your Son,
our Saviour Jesus Christ.

Dean Vaughan (adapted)

16th **For forgiveness**

Forgive me my sins, O Lord.
Forgive me the sins of my soul and
the sins of my body, my secret and
whispering sins, the sins that I have
done to please myself and the sins
that I have done to please others.
Forgive me those sins which I know,
and those which I know not.
Forgive them, O Lord, forgive them
all, in your great goodness.

Lancelot Andrewes (abridged)

November

17th   Using our talents

O God, help us to use the particular gifts
that you have given us:

To use our minds to study your
word, which will prevent us from
becoming small-minded.

To use our wills to do the
things we know we ought to do.

To give you thanks and praise,
which will give us courage.

When things go wrong, help us to
learn to laugh.
When we are reproved, may we be
grateful.
When we have failed, let us determine
to succeed.

St Hilda's Homily (adapted)

18th   In our need of grace

As a fish that is dragged from the
water gasps, so gasps my soul.
As one who has buried his treasure,
and now cannot find the place,
so is my mind distraught.
As child who has lost its mother,
so am I troubled.
my heart is seared with sore anguish.
O merciful God,
You know my need.
Come, save me and show me your love.

Tukaram

19th **For pardon**

O God, who loves us,
look with eyes of pity and compassion
on us your humble servants, who trust
in your unfailing love and who now
implore you to forgive us our sins,
through Jesus Christ our Lord, Amen.

Gelasian Sacramentary (adapted)

20th **Prayer for help**

Listen to me, Lord, and answer me,
for I am helpless and weak.

You are my God, so be merciful to me.
I pray to you all day long.
Make your servant glad, O Lord,
because my prayers go up to you.
You are good to us and forgiving,
full of constant love for all who
pray to you.

From Psalm 86

November

21st   **A cry for help**

O Lord,
you know what I long for;
you hear all my groans.
My heart is pounding,
my strength is gone, and
my eyes have lost their brightness.

But I trust in you, O Lord;
and you, O Lord my God, will answer
me.

Do not abandon me, O Lord;
do not stay away, my God!
Help me now, O Lord my saviour!

From Psalm 38

22nd   **Prayer for help**

Save me, O God!
Lord, help me now!

May all who come to you be glad and
joyful.
May all who are thankful for your
salvation always say,
'How great is God!'
I am weak and poor;
come to me quickly, O God.
You are my saviour;
O Lord, hurry to my aid!

From Psalm 70

23rd   **Longing for God**

O God, you are my God,
and I long for you.
My whole being desires you; like a
dry, worn-out and waterless land,
my soul is thirsty for you.

Let me see you in the sanctuary;
let me see how mighty and glorious
you are.

Your constant love is better than
life itself, and so I will praise you.
I will give thanks as long as I live;
I will raise my hands to you in
prayer.
My soul will feast and be satisfied,
and I will sing glad songs of praise
to you.

From Psalm 63

24th   **For eternal values**

O God,
help us not to mind earthly things,
but to love things heavenly.
And now, whilst we are living amongst
things which are passing away, help
us to cleave to those things which
are eternal, through Jesus Christ our
Lord, Amen.

Leonine Sacramentary (adapted)

November

25th   For God's Spirit

Lord,
open our eyes,
that we may see you in our
brothers and sisters.

Lord,
open our ears,
that we may hear the cries of the
hungry, the cold, the frightened, the
oppressed.

Lord,
open our hearts,
that we may love each other as you
love us.

Lord,
renew us in spirit,
that we may be free.

Co-workers of Mother Teresa (adapted)

26th   For receiving God's word

O Lord,
you have given us your word for a
light to shine upon our path;
help us so to meditate upon that
word, and to follow its teaching,
that we may find in it the light that
shines more and more until the
perfect day, through Jesus Christ our
Lord, Amen.

St Jerome

27th   **For God's light**

O God, our guide who goes before us,
shine your light upon us, so that
being rid of the darkness of our
hearts, we may attain to your true
light, through Jesus Christ, the
Light of the World, Amen.

Sarum Breviary (adapted)

28th   **For God's peace**

O God, my source of comfort and help,
drop your still dews of quietness,
till all my strivings cease.
Take from my soul the strain and
stress, and let my ordered life
confess the beauty of your peace,
Amen.

J. G. Whittier (adapted)

29th   **For the blessing of Jesus Christ**

Lord Jesus Christ,
be near me to defend me,
within me to refresh me,
around me to preserve me,
before me to guide me,
behind me to keep me on the right
path, and above me to bless me.

Anonymous, 10th century (adapted)

30th **On St Andrew's Day**

Almighty God,
who gave such grace to your apostle
Saint Andrew that he readily obeyed
the call of your Son and brought his
brother with him:
give us, who are called by your holy
Word, grace to follow without delay
and to tell the good news of your
kingdom; through Jesus Christ our
Lord, Amen.

Alternative Service Book

DECEMBER

The Word became a human being and, full of grace and truth, lived among us.   (John 1 : 14)

1st   **In praise of Christ**

> Joy to the world!
> The Lord is come.
> Let earth receive her king.
> Let every heart prepare him room
> And heaven and nature sing.

Isaac Watts

2nd   **For God's light and love**

> O God,
> have mercy on us and may your Holy
> Spirit illumine our inward souls, so
> as to kindle our cold hearts and
> light up our dark minds, Amen.

Mozarabic prayer (adapted)

3rd   **Preparation to receive Christ**

> O Lord our God,
> give us grace to desire you with a
> whole heart, so that desiring you,
> we may seek you and find you;
> and so finding you, may love you;
> and loving you may hate our
> selfishness that separates us from
> you.

St Anselm

December

4th   **For being ready to receive Christ**

Lord Jesus Christ,
open the ears and eyes of my heart,
that I may hear and understand your
Word and do your will.
I am a pilgrim on earth. Hide not
your commandments from me. Take away
the covering from my eyes, that I may
see wonderful things in your law.

Ephrem Syrus

5th   **Preparation to receive Christ**

O God,
Give me a clean heart ready to
receive the Lord Jesus, so that he
will be glad to come in, gratefully
accepting its hospitality.

Origen (adapted)

6th   **To be a light for Christ**

Almighty God,
Enlighten us with the light of your
Holy Spirit, that we may shine like
blazing lights in the presence of
your Son, Jesus Christ our Lord,
Amen.

Gelasian Sacramentary
(abridged and adapted)

7th **Adoration**

Ah Lord God, lover of my soul,
when you come into my soul, all that
is within me shall rejoice.
You are my glory and the exultation
of my heart.
You are my hope and refuge in the day
of my trouble.
Let me love you more than myself and
only love myself for you in me.

Thomas à Kempis
(abridged and adapted)

8th **Adoration, praise and intercession**

Jesus, my Lord,
come to me, comfort me, console me.
Visit the hearts in strange lands
who are yearning for you.
Visit the dying and those who have
died without you.

Jesus, my Lord,
visit also those who persecute you.
Lord Jesus, you are my light in the
darkness. You are my warmth in the
cold. You are my happiness in
sorrow.

Anonymous

December

9th   **For God's light and truth**

O Christ, Light of the World,
shine upon our minds and hearts.
O Christ, Spirit of Truth,
guide us into all truth,
for your love's sake, Amen.

L. Tuttiet (abridged)

10th   **For Christ's presence**

Come in, O Christ, and judge us.
Come and cast out from us every sin
that hinders you.
Come, purge our souls by your
presence.
Come, be our king for ever.

Bishop Phillips Brooks

11th   **For knowing God**

My God,
I pray that I may so know you and
love you that I may rejoice in you.
And if I may not do so fully in this
life, let me go steadily on to the
day when I come to that fullness.
Let me receive that which you have
promised through your truth, that my
joy may be full.

St Anselm

12th   **For receiving Christ**

Lord Christ,
open wide the window of my spirit
and fill me full of your light.
Open wide the door of my heart, that
I may receive you and entertain you
with all my powers of adoration and
love.

Christina Rossetti

13th   **For receiving Christ's love**

Lord Jesus, who is love incarnate,
show yourself to us who knock, that
knowing you, we may love you, desire
you and think always of you.
Awaken in us such a love as may
rightly and fittingly be given to
you.
O God, may your love take possession
of our whole being and make it
totally yours.

St Columbanus (adapted)

14th   **For receiving God**

O God our Creator and Father,
as the heavens are higher than the
earth, so are your ways higher than
our ways. How wonderful is your love
for each of us.
As Mary obeyed you and trusted you,
loved you and was made happy by the
birth of your Son, Jesus Christ, may
we through our obedience, trust and
love receive you into our hearts,
today and always, Amen.

P. N.

December

15th   Preparation for meeting Christ

Lord Jesus,
help us always to wait for you, to
wish for you and to watch for you, so
that at your coming again you may
find us ready.

Ancient collect (adapted)

16th   Self-dedication to Christ

To you, Lord Jesus,
I direct my eyes;
to you my hands,
to you my humble knees;
to you my heart shall offer
sacrifice;
to you my thoughts,
who my thoughts sees;
to you myself –
myself and all I give.
For you I die.
For you alone I live.

Attributed to Sir Walter Raleigh
(adapted)

17th   Giving myself to Christ

Lord Jesus,
I offer myself to you today,
to be your servant for ever,
to obey you and to love you always.

Thomas à Kempis (adapted)

18th   **Giving myself to Christ**

Living or dying, Lord, I would be
yours. Keep me your own for ever.
Draw me day by day nearer to you
until I am wholly filled with your
love.

E. B. Pusey (adapted)

19th   **Giving myself to Christ**

Lord Jesus,
I give myself to you.
I trust you completely.
You are wiser than I and you love me
more than I love myself.
Use me in whatever way you will.
I ask not to see. I ask not to know.
I simply ask to be used, for your
love's sake, Amen.

Cardinal Newman (adapted)

20th   **For God's gift to me this Christmas**

O loving Father,
who by the birth of your holy child
Jesus has given me a great light to
shine in my darkness, help me to see
light in his light till the end of my
days.
Give to me your most perfect
Christmas gift of love for all
people, so that your Son may be born
in me and I shall have the ever
brightening hope of eternal life with
you, through Jesus Christ our Lord,
Amen.

Professor Knight (adapted)

December

21st   **On St Thomas' Day**

Lord Christ,
you led your apostle Thomas through
his doubts to complete faith in you.
Help us in our lack of faith to learn
to entrust ourselves into your care,
Amen.

P. N.

22nd   **A gift for Christ**

What can I give him, poor as I am?
If I were a shepherd, I would bring a
lamb. If I were a wise man, I would
do my part.
What can I give him? Give my heart.

Christina Rossetti

23rd   **Christmas prayer**

Grant us, O God, such love and wonder
that with the humble shepherds, wise
men and pilgrims unknown, we may come
and adore the Holy Babe, the Heavenly
King; and with our gifts, worship and
serve him, our Lord and Saviour Jesus
Christ.

James Ferguson

24th   **For welcoming Jesus at Christmas**

Lord Jesus,
Help me to welcome you this Christmas
not in the cold manger of my heart,
but in a heart full of love and
humility, a heart warm with love for
others.

Mother Teresa (adapted)

25th   **On Christmas Day**

Make me pure, Lord: Thou art holy.
Make me meek, Lord: Thou wert lowly.
Now beginning and alway;
Now begin, on Christmas Day.

Gerard Manley Hopkins

December

26th   **On St Stephen's Day**

Lord Jesus,
we give thanks for your first martyr
Stephen and for all who have suffered
for their faith in you.
Give us courage in the face of
adversity.
Help us to forgive our enemies and to
pray for them.
Into your hands we commit our spirit,
now and always, Amen.

P. N.

27th   **On St John the Evangelist's Day**

Merciful Father,
whose Son is the light of the world:
so guide your Church by the teaching
of your apostle and evangelist Saint
John, that we may walk by the light
that has come among us and finally
know him as the light of everlasting
life; who is alive and reigns with
you and the Holy Spirit, one God,
now and for ever, Amen.

Alternative Service Book

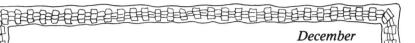

28th   **For the Holy Innocents**

Heavenly Father,
whose children suffered at the hands
of Herod, though they had done no
wrong:
give us grace neither to act cruelly
nor to stand indifferently by, but to
defend the weak from the tyranny of
the strong; in the name of Jesus
Christ who suffered for us, but is
alive and reigns with you and the
Holy Spirit, one God, now and for
ever, Amen.

Alternative Service Book

29th   **For peace on earth**

O God,
in my despair I bowed my head.
'There is no peace on earth,' I said.
For hate is strong and mocks the song
of 'peace on earth, goodwill to men'.
Then pealed the bells more loud and
deep. God is not dead, nor does he
sleep. The wrong shall fail, the
right prevail with peace on earth,
goodwill to men.

H. W. Longfellow

30th   Self-dedication to Christ

Lord Jesus
I give you my hands to do your work.
I give you my feet to go your way.
I give you my eyes to see as you do.
I give you my tongue to speak your
words.
I give you my mind that you may think
in me.
I give you my spirit that you may
pray in me.
Above all, I give you my heart that
you may love in me your Father and
all mankind.
I give you my whole self that you may
grow in me, so that it is you, Lord
Jesus, who live and work and pray in
me.

Grail Prayer

31st   For Christ's coming

God be in my head and in my
understanding.
God be in my eyes and in my looking.
God be in my mouth and in my
speaking.
God be in my heart and in my
thinking.
God be at my end and at my departing.

Sarum Primer

ACKNOWLEDGEMENTS

In 1978, I inherited from my aunt and godmother, Sophy Tiarks, *A Chain of Prayer across the Ages, Forty Centuries of Prayer 2000 BC - AD 1923*, compiled and arranged for daily use by Selina Fitzherbert Fox, M.D., B.S. It was published by John Murray and had appeared first in 1913. My aunt's copy was a fifth edition reprinted in June 1933; it was so well used that it was falling to bits. Because of its old-fashioned style, *A Chain of Prayer across the Ages* does not have modern appeal, but the thoughts expressed by the prayers that it includes are just as relevant to us today as they were then. I have used many of these prayers in modernised form.

I have also drawn on *The Hodder Book of Christian Prayers*, compiled by Tony Castle, Hodder and Stoughton, 1986; *God of a Hundred Names*, compiled by Barbara Green and Victor Gollancz, published by Victor Gollancz, 1982; *The Alternative Service Book*, 1980; *The Book of Common Prayer*, 1662; *The Good News Bible*, 1976; *The Oxford Book of Prayer*, OUP, 1985; *In the Silence of the Heart*, by Mother Teresa, SPCK, 1983; *Prayers for Pastoral Occasions*, compiled by Michael Mayne, Mowbray, 1982; *Enfolded in Love*, daily readings with Julian of Norwich, Darton Longman and Todd, 1980; *Prayers from a Troubled Heart* by George Appleton, Darton Longman and Todd, 1983; *A Calendar of Prayer*, compiled by Fiona Macmath, Marshall Pickering, 1988; *Parish Prayers*, edited by Frank Colquhoun, Hodder and Stoughton, 1967; and *Prayers for use at the Alternative Services*, compiled by David Silk, Mowbray, 1980. I wish to express my thanks to all these compilers and publishers.

The artistic design, which is the work of Joanna Queen, is an important part of this book. The border designs are based on embroidery stitches and helped me to choose the title of the book. I know that Joanna's illustrations were born out of much prayer, thoughtfulness and hard work, for which I thank her very much. Also I am grateful to my father, Philip Mayne, for his help in compiling the index and to my husband, David, for his many suggestions and for much practical help in bringing the manuscript to publication. Without David's love, help and encouragement this book would not have been completed.

I have tried to identify and trace all copyright material and obtain the necessary permissions. If I have unwittingly appropriated the work of others without acknowledgement, I apologise sincerely and will acknowledge any such oversights at the first opportunity. I acknowledge with thanks permisson to reproduce copyright material as listed below.

Augsburg Fortress Publishers for prayers from the U.S. edition of *Prayers from a Troubled Heart* by George Appleton (1983).

Bible text is reproduced from *The Good News Bible*, copyright of The American Bible Society, New York 1966, 1971 and 4th edition 1976, published by The Bible Societies / Harper Collins, with permission.

The British Broadcasting Corporation for prayers from *New Every Morning* (1973).

Cambridge University Press for extracts based on *The Book of Common Prayer* of 1662, the rights in which are vested in the Crown in perpetuity within the United Kingdom.

The Central Board of Finance of the Church of England for extracts from the *Alternative Service Book* (1980).

The Dean and Chapter of Durham Cathedral for the prayer 'On St Cuthbert's Day' displayed in Durham Cathedral.

Edward England Books for extracts from *The Hodder Book of Christian Prayers* (1986) compiled by Tony Castle.

Victor Gollancz Ltd for extracts from *God of a Hundred Names* (1962) collected and arranged by Barbara Greene and Victor Gollancz.

Longman Group UK for an adapted version of 'Life with God' by Eric Milner White from *The Cambridge Bede Book*.

Marshall Pickering for 'Christmas Prayer' by James Ferguson published in *A Calendar of Prayer* (1988) - an anthology of classic prayers compiled by Fiona MacMath.

McCrimmon Publishing Company Ltd for extracts from *You must be joking, Lord.*

A. R. Mowbray & Co. Ltd (a division of Cassell plc) for extracts from *Prayers for Pastoral Occasions* (1982) compiled by Michael Mayne.

Oxford University Press for two prayers by George Appleton: 'For the gift of sight' and 'For peace' reprinted from *The Oxford Book of Prayer* edited by George Appleton (1985).

The Rt Revd Lord Runcie of Cuddesdon for the prayer *For reverence of life.*

Sheed & Ward, Kansas City, Missouri for 'When we feel we have no time' by Michel Quoist in *Prayers* (1963).

SPCK for prayers by Mother Teresa and her co-workers from *In the Silence of the Heart* (1983), edited by Kathryn Spink.

Templegate Publishers for prayers from the U.S. edition of *Enfolded in Love* (1980), Daily Readings with Julian of Norwich.

In the case of other material used, efforts to contact the copyright-holders have not been successful.

INDEX

Prayers are identified by the designation: month/day

Another Book for
Daily Reflection and Prayer
from Servant Publications

Grace in Every Season
Through the Year with Catherine Doherty
Daily Reflections Selected by
Mary Achterhoff

This rich seasonal devotional reads like a sampler of the everyday spirituality of Catherine Doherty—a spiritual giant of the twentieth century who counted Thomas Merton and Dorothy Day among her friends, founded the Madonna House Apostolate, and left extensive writings to her spiritual sons and daughters. There are mystical poems about birth and death and homespun words of advice on work and home life. Nostalgic entries even recall Christmas and Easter customs from Catherine's childhood in the Old Russia of the czars.

Grace in Every Season provides an excellent introduction to Catherine Doherty's spirituality and a wide selection of her writings that will be of interest to her many spiritual children. *$9.99*